Overcoming Problems

Effective Steps and Strategies to Create Your Blockbuster Life

Sally Learey

Overcoming Problems

Effective Steps and Strategies to Create Your Blockbuster Life

Sally Learey

B.A. (Sociology), Dip. T. (Prim & Sec), Cert. 1V Training and Assessment, Dip. Professional Counselling

Published in 2012 by
Sandcastle Press
PO Box 748, Belmont, Vic 3216
sandcastlepress@optusnet.com.au
Text & illustrations copyright © Sally Learey 2012

Every effort has been made to ensure that this book is free from error or omissions. However,
the Publisher, the Author, the Illustrator, the Editor, or their respective employees or agents, shall not
accept responsibility for injury, loss or damage occasioned to any person acting or refraining from
action as a result of material in this book whether or not such injury, loss or damage is in any way due
to any negligent act or omission, breach of duty or default on the part of the Publisher, the Author,
the Illustrator, the Editor, or their respective employees or agents.

Design and typeset by Mudgroup
Illustrations by Stuart Craven
Author photographs by Tremayne Photography
Printed and bound by 1010 Printing

National Library of Australia
Cataloguing -in- Publication entry:

Learey, Sally.
Overcoming Problems.
ISBN 9780980344165 (pbk.)
Problem solving.
Reasoning.

153.43

This book is dedicated to you, the reader.

Take action and create the blockbuster life that you deserve.

"Everyone thinks of changing the world, but no one thinks of changing himself."

Leo Tolstoy (Russian Novelist, 1828-1910)

Acknowledgement

Most of the complex problems I have overcome in the last fifteen years have been health related. I have always fought for a correct diagnosis for one reason and one reason only; to gain understanding and move forward. For me, a diagnosis is not a label or stigma. Rather, it's a guiding light to empowerment and wellness.

This book is a legacy to those last fifteen years of my life. The skills, strengths and knowledge I have gained are momentous. The commitment and resourcefulness necessary to overcome major challenge after major challenge has been beyond imagination. And yet my life is now richer.

To all those friends and professionals who years ago planted the seed of writing this book, then watered it and continued watering it, with comment and suggestion as each new challenge emerged. As you well know, the challenges have been both relentless and back to back, so much so that the seed has become a tree (a snow gum, my favourite tree) and I can ignore it no longer! Thank you for your belief in me.

To David, Emily, Caitlin and Lachlan – your confidence in me to overcome the most complex of challenges has been remarkable. We did it (and keep doing it) together;

To my near and dear friends for your unconditional love and support;

To Allison and Jo for proofreading;

To Jacinta for your invaluable input;

To Meg for your knowledge, compassion and respect;

My heart felt thanks to you all.

I would like to acknowledge all the bright minded people whose insightful thoughts appear as quotes in this book. Their wisdom is timeless. The world is a better place because they walked this earth.

"Sweet are the uses of adversity which, like the toad, ugly and venomous, wears yet a precious jewel in his head."

William Shakespeare (From the Play 'As You Like It')
(English Dramatist, 1564-1616)

"All misfortune is but a stepping stone to fortune."
Henry David Thoreau (American Writer, 1817-1862)

Contents

Chapter 3 : Types of Problems

Chapter 4 : A Practical Approach

Chapter 5 : Lessons to Learn

Chapter 6 : Behaviours and Emotional States to Embrace

Chapter 7 : Behaviours and Emotional States to Minimise

Chapter 8 : Looking After Yourself

Chapter 9 : Finding The Magnificence In Problems

Chapter 10 : All About You

Foreword

As a psychologist I see many people with hiccups, challenges and crises through their lives. How people deal with these issues can be an indication of what the future holds for them.

Sally Learey has had more than her fair share of challenges in life however she not only seems to rise above them but turns them into opportunities. When two of her children were diagnosed with coeliac disease she somehow managed to find the energy to write her first children's book, Food For Me Is Gluten Free, and made a difference for many families experiencing the gluten free journey. Since then she has gone from strength to strength as an author.

In this book Sally has successfully combined psychological constructs with the insight of Buddhism and the wisdom of various philosophers and writers to create an easy-to-read book about problem solving. The *8 steps* emphasise that choice, not chance, determines the outcome of the situation. What's more, once a solution is found the problem is not actually solved. Constant review and checking is required.

Her suggestions that we reflect on past decisions with curiosity rather than judgement and that we all need to deal with minor problems quickly otherwise they will grow, show insight and understanding of these complex issues. Her practical suggestions are also excellent. After all, when feeling overwhelmed by the problem it is incredibly difficult to generate ideas about how to stay focused or to determine what coping strategies to employ.

Overall Sally has reminded us to take control of our lives, recognise our skills and be kind to ourselves. And there may be times in life for all of us when we need to call on every problem solving resource available to us, just as she has done.

Meg Wardlaw
Psychologist

Chapter 1
All About Problems

The benefits of problem solving

"The man who has no more problems to solve is out of the game."
Elbert Hubbard (American Writer and Philosopher, 1856-1915)

Problems are a part of life. You can either let problems overcome you or you can overcome problems. It's your choice.

> ➤ Just think what you could achieve, if you stopped putting your life on hold whenever a problem appeared.
> ➤ Imagine managing every challenge you faced with confidence.
> ➤ How great would you feel knowing you are in control of your own life and your own happiness, because you hold the key to problem solving?

Essentially *every aspect of your life* is affected by your ability to problem-solve. Shaping your own experiences, achieving your personal and professional goals and living a blockbuster life *are within your reach*, once you learn how to overcome your problems efficiently and effectively!

Problems are subjective

"If all misfortunes were laid in one common heap whence everyone must take an equal portion, most people would be contented to take their own and depart."

Socrates (Greek Philosopher, 469-399 B.C.)

In life, there are no universal problems. What's a problem to you is not necessarily a problem to another person. So you need to define what a problem is *for you*.

The nature of problems can vary dramatically from person to person. We are all different and we all bring a mix of genetics, perspectives and life experiences to the situations we face. That's what makes us unique.

According to the World Book Dictionary, a problem can be: 'a question, especially a difficult question, a matter of doubt or difficulty, something to be worked out or something that causes trouble or difficulty'.

You can substitute the word problem for many other words such as:

- challenge
- difficulty
- situation
- issue
- crisis
- dilemma
- predicament
- quandary
- hitch
- trouble.

A different choice of word may change your view of the problem in question, so choose the word that works the best for you.

Once you have defined something in your life as a problem, the next step is to overcome it.

Problem solving exposed

"I am, indeed, a king, because I know how to rule myself."
Pietro Aretino (Italian Poet, 1492-1556)

You problem-solve every day. Many times you don't even realise it. *Solving repetitive problems*, such as what will you eat for breakfast, what time will you leave for work and what will you do when your child throws a tantrum, are all part of routine problem solving – they seem so familiar that you don't consciously comprehend you are problem solving when you make these decisions. You are on auto-pilot. Your problem solving is occurring at the *unconscious* level. These decisions have in fact become *habits*.

Examine these habitual responses from time to time by becoming consciously aware of what you say or do. Once you have this awareness, you can determine whether your current habits really are the best solutions to your repetitive problems or whether you should put some time and thought into finding *better solutions*.

Solving new or different problems requires a strategic type of problem solving. This involves following a series of *logical steps*. These steps act as a guide, leading you to ask powerful questions so you can discover and implement the best solutions to your problems. These steps also act as a source of help and motivation if you become stuck, unsure of what to do, or disillusioned with the problem solving process.

Solving complicated problems necessitates an additional set of skills. Sustained thinking, the ability to regulate your emotions and the capacity to make and follow through with tough decisions are just some of these skills. Armed with this type of empowering *skill set*, you will be able to see your complicated problems through to solutions in spite of the following types of *barriers*:

- feeling overwhelmed
- believing the negative thoughts circulating in your head
- focusing on and worrying constantly about your problem
- choosing a solution that doesn't end up solving your problem.

Overcoming problems is a *process* that needs to be *planned*. But unfortunately for many people, problem solving is left to a process of hit and miss. It ends up being dependent on things like mood, energy levels or what's on T.V. Sometimes it's about more than that. It's about *not knowing what to do*!

The good news is that if you want to overcome problems efficiently and effectively, with the best possible outcomes every single time, you *can*! The secret is to *learn how*!

Chapter 2

The 8 Steps to Overcoming Problems

The 8 steps

"By failing to prepare you are preparing to fail."

Benjamin Franklin (American Politician, 1706-1790)

There are *8 steps* to overcoming a problem. These *8 steps* are easy to apply. They are also easy to learn. You can remember the *8 steps* by using the acronym **'ACT TODAY'**.

The *8 steps to overcoming problems* are:

'ACT TODAY'

1. **A**ware of and admit to having a problem

2. **C**larify the problem

3. **T**ime to ask quality questions

4. **T**he thinking phase

5. **O**ne solution stands out

6. **D**ecisions for your solution

7. **A**ct on and review your solution

8. **Y**our reward.

These *8 steps to overcoming problems* are universal. They can *consistently* be applied to every problem you encounter. Each step is simple, yet powerful.

As you work through the *8 steps* prepare to…

1. *Challenge yourself*
2. *Move out of your comfort zone*
3. *Do what is necessary mentally, emotionally, spiritually, physically and behaviorally*

…so you can achieve the best possible solution to your problem.

When cycling through these *8 steps* becomes automatic, you will have mastered the art of overcoming problems.

Step 1: Aware and admit

"It isn't that they can't see the solution. It is that they can't see the problem."
Gilbert K. Chesterton (English Writer, 1874-1936)

Adopt an *awareness* of what's going on *around you* and *within you.* When you open your eyes and open your heart, you can sense if things are not right. If you identify an issue, draw attention to it. Admit to yourself that there is a problem, when there is a problem. You can't overcome something if you won't admit its existence. Admitting there is a problem is a sign of strength and insight. It really is!

Admitting there is a problem *does not mean admitting you are the problem.* People think they are one and the same. They are not.

You are a human being and human beings have problems. That's a fact. So do not be ashamed of problems. The only shame would come from being unable to admit that you have problems.

➤ How can you grow if you don't expand your mind?
➤ How can you learn new skills?
➤ How can you engage fully in life if you can't be honest with yourself?

If you have a problem, admit it, and get on with the process of overcoming it.

Step 1 in action

I am aware that I have put on weight recently. I can't fit comfortably into my clothes. To be honest, I can't zip up some of my trousers. After having a long, hard look at myself in the mirror I admit that I am overweight.

Step 2: Clarify the problem

"No problem can be solved until it is reduced to some simple form. The changing of a vague difficulty into a specific, concrete form is a very essential element in thinking."

J.P. Morgan (American Financier and Banker, 1837-1913)

Take some time to think through your problem. Ask yourself the following question:

"What is the problem that I need to solve?"

Answer this question by stating the problem to yourself in plain and simple language. Write the problem down, type it out, say it out loud, say it in your mind; do whatever works for you so you can *clarify* and *process* the problem that you need to overcome.

The message is straightforward – *be very clear about what you are solving.*

If necessary, make a date with yourself to clarify problems. Write it in your diary and then follow through.

When you can see your problems clearly, it's a lot easier to create momentum around solving them.

Step 2 in action

I have put on 10 kilograms and I can't fit into my clothes.

Once you have clarified a problem, *now* is the time to begin solving it. Don't wait until tomorrow – tomorrow never comes. Start working on it *today*. Launch into asking some quality questions. Remember: **'ACT TODAY'!**

Step 3: Time to ask quality questions

"A prudent question is one-half of wisdom."

Francis Bacon (English Lawyer and Philosopher, 1561-1626)

Asking better questions is the starting point to overcoming problems. It's the secret to putting yourself in a creative, positive, productive, *solution focused* headspace.

Asking better questions or *quality* questions lets you use your own knowledge and experience as a resource.

Quality questions are *open* questions. Open questions are questions that are phrased to encourage reflective thought.

Asking quality questions produces quality answers.

Quality questions in this 3rd step of the problem solving process are *'what'* questions.

Here are some examples of these 'open, quality, what' questions.

- What aspects of this problem do I need to get under control?
- What does this problem need?
- What are my non-negotiable behaviours when solving this problem?

- What are some possible solutions to this problem?
- What needs to be *done* to solve it?
- What needs to be *said* to solve it?
- What past experiences can I draw on?
- What can I learn from the experience of others that can help me overcome this problem?
- What do I *need* right now to deal with this problem?
- What strengths do I need to help me solve this problem?
- What part of the problem do I still need to grasp?
- What are the questions that I haven't asked?
- What's good about this problem?
- What lessons can I learn from this problem?

You can use this set of quality questions every time you have a problem to overcome. These questions can move your problem towards a solution by *setting thought in motion.*

Step 3 in action

What aspects of putting on weight do I need to get under control?

What do I need to do about not being able to fit into my clothes?

What are my non-negotiable behaviours about dealing with my weight gain?

What are some possible solutions to my problem of weight gain?

What needs to be done about my weight gain?

What needs to be said about my weight gain?

What past weight gain experiences can I draw on?

What can I learn from the experience of others that can help me?

What do I need right now to deal with my weight gain problem?

What strengths do I need to help me solve my weight gain problem?

What part of my weight gain problem do I still need to grasp?

What are the questions that I haven't asked?

What's good about my weight gain?

What lessons can I learn from my weight gain?

Step 4: The thinking phase

"No problem can withstand the assault of sustained thinking."

Voltaire (French poet and philosopher, 1694-1778)

As you ask quality questions, your unconscious mind will get to work thinking of possible answers. At the same time, you can put your conscious mind to work thinking of possible answers...

If your problem is major or complex, you may need to give it extra time, extra focus and extra investigation so you can think of possible answers.

The following strategies may help:
- researching on the internet
- reading books
- consulting a counsellor
- using the wealth of knowledge and experience that you already have from past situations
- asking trusted people for ideas
- seeking out experts if you require a specific type of information such as medical or legal knowledge
- tuning in to your intuition
- asking yourself quality questions over and over again.

Remember, you are thinking of possible solutions, so record all your ideas as possibilities.

A powerful strategy when asking yourself questions is to record both the questions and the answers. That way your brain has a better chance of processing all the information clearly and accurately.

Step 4 in action

What aspects of putting on weight do I need to get under control?
I need to take responsibility for my weight gain. I need to consider my lifestyle.

What do I need to do about not being able to fit into my clothes?
I need to lose weight. I need to buy a new wardrobe of larger sized clothes.

What are my non-negotiable behaviours about dealing with my weight gain?
I need to make a commitment to losing weight.
I need to listen to my self-talk and make it proactive and encouraging.

What are some possible solutions to my problem of weight gain?
Exercise. Eat smaller meal portions. Make healthier food choices.
Join a gym. Hire a food coach. Consult a dietician.

What needs to be done about my weight gain?
I need to examine my eating habits. I need to start an exercise program.
I need to monitor my weight weekly.

What needs to be said about my weight gain?
"*I have put on 10 kilos and now I'm going to focus on losing it.*"

What past weight gain experiences can I draw on?
I need to lose weight gradually via a sensible eating plan and regular exercise.

What can I learn from the experience of others that can help me?
Make myself accountable to someone else.

What do I need right now to deal with my weight gain problem?
I need a friend to support me. I need to join a gym.
I need to plan for healthy meals, shop for fresh ingredients and eat a healthy diet.

What strengths do I need to help me solve my weight gain problem?
Perseverance. Courage. Commitment. Self-control. Patience. Self-belief.

What part of my weight gain problem do I still need to grasp?
I am responsible for my weight gain and my weight loss.

What are the questions that I haven't asked?
How long will it take to lose 10 kilos? How will I avoid future weight gain?

What's good about my weight gain?
I can role model to my children how to overcome a weight gain problem.

What lessons can I learn from my weight gain?
I can learn to pay attention to my weight and health.

Step 5: One solution stands out

"Choose always the way that seems the best, however rough it may be; custom will soon render it easy and agreeable."

Pythagoras (Greek Mathematician and Philosopher, 580-500 B.C.)

Sooner or later, depending on the nature and context of your problem, you will need to decide on a solution. So *evaluate* the possible solutions you identified during the *thinking phase.*

Think about them from all angles:

- ➤ mental
- ➤ emotional
- ➤ social
- ➤ physical
- ➤ financial
- ➤ practical
- ➤ short term
- ➤ long term.

There could be an extremely obvious solution, or you may need to make another investment of time and thought until one solution stands out for you as the 'best'.

It is important to remember that you are not looking for the easiest solution. You are looking for the solution that will overcome your problem in the *best* possible way. Odds are it will not be the easiest one. It may even be the hardest.

When you are ready, go ahead and choose a solution!

Feel confident about your choice.

Your thoughts, feelings and behaviours will align with it.

You may even feel a sense of relief in your mind, body and soul, particularly if your problem has been long standing or your solution was hard to come by. This relief is a releasing of tension and pent up emotion, of uncertainty and self doubt. It's a good thing.

Step 5 in action

I will join a gym.

You can now focus all your energy on *applying* the solution you have chosen…

Step 6: Decisions for your solution

"Choices are the hinges of destiny."

Pythagoras (Greek Mathematician and Philosopher, 580-500 B.C.)

Now that you have chosen a solution to your problem, please realise that your problem is *not yet solved*! Many people make the mistake of thinking that it is.

Deciding on a solution does not necessarily include deciding *how to apply* and *when to apply* that solution. These are extra decisions that must be made.

That's what *this step* of the problem solving process is all about…

1. Deciding *how* to apply your solution.

2. Deciding *when* to apply your solution.

Asking quality questions will once again support you in thinking about possible answers.

Quality questions in this 6th step are *'how'* and *'when'* questions.

Here are some examples of these 'how' and 'when' questions.

- How can I apply my solution in the most effective way?
- How can I use my time, energy and skills to apply my solution?

- How will I tell other people about my solution?
- How can I apply my solution whilst causing the least amount of hurt to others?
- How will I manage my emotions when I apply my solution?
- How will I manage the emotional responses of others when I apply my solution?
- How will I cope if other people criticise my solution?
- When will I apply my solution?
- When will I tell other people about my solution?

  (Keep in mind that some of these questions may only be relevant to complex, major and painful problems.)

Set yourself a *timeframe* to decide *how* and *when* to apply your solution to your problem.

(Note that when you need to make *instant* decisions your timeframe will be *immediate.*)

When time is up, *make your decisions*!

Commit to them.

Lock them in.

Make them non-negotiable.

Trust your judgement.

Don't look back.

These decisions are *right for you* because *you* made them.

Feel empowered knowing it is *choice*, not chance, that determines the *what, how* and *when* of overcoming *your* problems.

Step 6 in action

How can I apply my solution in the most effective way?
I will phone two local gyms tomorrow and ask about their facilities. I will visit them both within the next two days in my lunch break/during the evening. I will make a decision by the end of the week and join the gym of my choice.

How can I use my time, energy and skills to apply my solution?
Each Sunday, Tuesday and Thursday night, I will organise all my workout gear. I will set my alarm for 6.00am on Monday, Wednesday and Friday mornings. When my alarm goes off, I will get straight out of bed and get dressed for the gym. I will drive to the gym and workout for an hour from 6.15am-7.15am.

How will I tell other people about my solution?
I will tell people how excited I am about my new exercise program.

How can I apply my solution whilst causing the least amount of hurt to others?

Going to the gym early in the mornings will have the least impact on others.
I will get organised for the next day, the night before.

How will I manage my emotions when I apply my solution?

I will be aware of any negative emotions and not let them affect my gym commitment.

I will manage my emotions by reframing when necessary.
I will go to bed an hour earlier each night to catch up on the sleep I'm missing through my early waking.

How will I manage the emotional responses of others when I apply my solution?

If they are positive responses, I will use them for motivation. If they are negative responses, I will ignore them.

How will I cope if other people criticise my solution?

I will remind myself of the strengths I need to use to see my solution through.
I will not let myself be affected by other people's negative or critical responses.

When will I apply my solution?

I will join a gym by the end of the week and start working out next Monday.
I will ask one of the gym instructors to help me set a timeframe in which to lose 10 kilograms. I will then use this date to measure the success of my solution.

When will I tell other people about my solution?

I will tell the people who I know will support me as soon as possible.
I will tell other people if or when the need arises.

Step 7: Act and review

"Knowing is not enough; we must apply. Willing is not enough; we must do."
Johann Wolfgang Goethe (German Poet, 1749-1832)

You have made some decisions. Congratulations. Now it's time to act on them!

This part of the *8 steps* can be both exciting and frightening. Keep your motivation level high.

If you are acting on your solution *immediately*, you must *act now!*
Put your solution into action!

If you are not acting immediately, then when the *designated time* comes you must *act! Put your solution into action!*

After you have put your solution into action, you need to check that your problem is solved. In other words, you need to *review* the outcome of your action.

This is one of the golden rules in problem solving, but many people neglect it.

So *review your action, review your action and review your action.*

Check that it provided you with the solution you were after.

Reviewing your action involves asking yourself some questions.

1. Have I solved the problem?
2. Am I happy with the solution?
3. Have I solved the entire problem or just some of it?
4. Do I need to take any further action in order to solve the problem?
5. What action do I need to take?
6. How will I take this action?
7. When will I take this action?

Reviewing and *taking further action* after choosing an original solution is not a shortfall. It's an intelligent move, if your original solution did not solve your problem satisfactorily. You are simply *taking the next step*. Prepare yourself to try a second solution or a third or even a fourth and so on.

An effective example of 'act and review' is how an airline pilot reaches his destination after take-off.

Despite planning, preparation, and many prior flights to the same destination, a pilot will modify his flight path, continuously if need be, due to unpredictable circumstances such as air turbulence and changing weather conditions. This pattern of adopting a chosen flight path followed by subsequent *reviews* is part of the pilot's job. His destination does not alter. The *flight path* he takes to get there does. By reviewing the plane's progress and making all the necessary adjustments, the pilot lands the flight on time on the designated runway. Great problem solving in action!

Failing to review actions is the undoing of many people. Problems sit there half solved or not solved properly, perpetuating a faulty mindset that problem solving just doesn't work!   This then becomes a self-fulfilling prophecy. So *beware*!

Step 7 in action

Have I solved the problem?
A weekly review of my weight loss will be an indicator as well as whether or not my clothes are fitting me more comfortably.

Am I happy with the solution?
I am enjoying the gym and seeing results so I am happy with my solution.

Have I solved the entire problem or just some of it?
I am working towards solving the entire problem within a given timeframe.

Do I need to take any further action in order to solve the problem?

I need to get my workouts reviewed and updated every fortnight by one of the gym instructors so I can keep challenging myself.

I need to review my diet so I can maximise my weight loss.

What action do I need to take?

I need to book a workout review every fortnight at the gym.

I need to book a consultation with a food coach at the gym.

I need to buy some new cookbooks with lots of low fat tasty meal ideas so I don't get bored with my new diet.

How will I take this action?

I will phone the gym and book a workout review appointment and a food coach appointment.

I will buy some cookbooks and cook 2 new meals per week.

When will I take this action?

I will phone the gym tomorrow.

I will buy 2 cookbooks this weekend.

Step 8: Your reward

"Obstacles are great incentives."
Jules Michelet (French Historian, 1798-1874)

Overcoming problems can be difficult. Sometimes the process can be long, challenging and confronting. That's why it's important to *acknowledge* what you have *achieved* when the problem has been solved! A reward is an ideal way of doing this.

Rewards can be both *intrinsic* and *extrinsic*. Intrinsic rewards are the greatest form of self-acknowledgement. They are felt internally. They are intangible. They are priceless.

Intrinsic rewards are things such as:
- the uplifting feeling of success that is experienced within
- a sense of satisfaction and achievement
- feeling proud
- feeling an increase in self-belief/courage/determination
- believing your positive self-talk
- being in the moment
- feeling worthwhile.

To discover your intrinsic rewards ask yourself the following questions about your problem solving experience.

1. How do I feel?
2. What have I achieved?
3. What did I do well?
4. What have I learnt?
5. What was the lesson in this problem?
6. What is the opportunity in this problem?
7. How can I make a difference to others beyond this problem?

Extrinsic rewards are gifts or experiences that you give to yourself. They are external to you. Extrinsic rewards are countless and varied. They are personally tailored. Whatever makes you feel good! Extrinsic rewards have the most impact when they are used sparingly. Save them for when you overcome a really challenging problem.

Some examples of (my) extrinsic rewards are:

- a new item of clothing
- a bottle of wine
- coffee and cake
- dinner out
- going to a movie
- a massage
- a facial.

No matter what the problem or how easy or difficult it was to overcome, remember to acknowledge your accomplishment!

Step 8 in action

My intrinsic rewards are my sense of pride, my sense of achievement and how wonderfully alive I feel.

My extrinsic reward is being able to fit into my clothes again!

Chapter 3

Types of Problems

Everyday or minor problems

"Have you got a problem?
Do what you can where you are with what you've got."
Theodore Roosevelt (American President, 1858-1919)

Some problems are minor and some problems are major. Your *perception* will determine whether a problem is *minor* or *major*. Perceptions differ from person to person, so what's minor for you may be major for someone else, or visa versa. Your perception will be right for you, so use it as your guide.

Minor problems should be dealt with quickly. If left too long, minor problems grow in size. Dwelling negatively upon a problem feeds it. The more focus and attention you give it, the larger it becomes *in your mind*. And before you know it, you will have a major problem on your hands.

You can solve minor or everyday problems as they arise, by learning *to think on your feet.* Work through the *8 steps to overcoming problems* mentally or jot down your thoughts. Your time constraints will determine how detailed the process can be. If you have the luxury of time, use it. Time allows you to be more focused, more disciplined and more thorough as you work your way through the **'ACT TODAY'** acronym. Even five minutes can be valuable. If time is not available, solve the problem in the moment.

Asking yourself the following two questions *now* will help you to progress through *the 8 steps to overcoming problems* when time is critical.

1. How will I work my way through the *8 steps to overcoming problems* on the spot?

Consider the following:

- talk myself through the *8 steps* in my mind
- talk myself through the *8 steps* out loud
- work my way through the *8 steps* using mental pictures/visuals
- work my way through the *8 steps* in a physical sense using the space around me.

2. How will I evaluate possibilities and choose a solution on the spot?

Consider the following:

- think in words
- think in pictures
- think in feelings
- think in actions.

Such preparation will pave the way for you to solve everyday problems with confidence and ease. (And leave panic and headaches far behind!)

Painful problems

"We cannot learn without pain."
Aristotle (Greek Philosopher, 384-322 B.C.)

Being human means you experience emotions. Some emotions uplift you, others drag you down and others lie somewhere in between.

Overcoming some types of problems is *emotionally painful*. Pain is an emotion that reflects *loss*. Dealing with loss always takes time as it involves *grief*. Grief is bound up in its own process of stages. If you are overcoming a problem associated with emotional pain, acknowledge your feelings and be kind to yourself. Realise that the *8 steps to overcoming problems* still apply to your problem. Be mindful that the *8 steps* offer guidance and support.

When you are dealing with a problem entwined in emotional pain remind yourself of the following.

1. Your attitude is very important.
2. You are taking action to work through the problem.
3. The feelings you are experiencing will pass.

It's a cliché, I know, but time really is the best healer.

Far reaching, complex or major problems

*"Divide each difficulty into as many parts as is feasible
and necessary to resolve it."*

René Descartes (French Mathematician, 1596-1650)

Don't stop living when you have a major problem to overcome. I know this is easier said than done, especially when your whole world *feels* like it's crashing down around you. As problems are a part of life, knowing how you can effectively problem-solve, *whilst* continuing to live your life productively, is the key.

Overcoming major problems is a journey. You will need to use the *8 steps to overcoming problems* repeatedly. That's because your major problem will consist of smaller step-by-step sequential problems. At times, it may seem as though you're going backwards. Assure yourself that you are not. It is helpful to have foresight. Yes, you are solving one piece of the major problem after another piece. And yes, when you have solved a smaller problem you may still feel surrounded by the next problem and the next. But the big picture is important. *Reflect* on what you have resolved so far and acknowledge that you are making headway.

You may need to call on *every* problem solving resource available to you. That's being smart, practical and creative. If you need to, do it. I know I have. That's how the ideas for this book evolved.

Another way to tackle major problems is by taking one massive bite and chewing like there's no tomorrow. In other words, forget working in smaller bite sized problems and just solve the problem in one fell swoop. Sounds time efficient doesn't it? The danger with this method is that it's riddled with potential pitfalls, such as:

➤ performing each problem solving step poorly
➤ suffering fatigue trying to reach a solution in a short space of time
➤ becoming disheartened as suddenly the problem seems far too big for you to manage
➤ only solving part of the problem because you did not clarify it effectively
➤ applying a solution only to find that is wasn't the best solution to choose
➤ losing confidence in your problem solving ability.

Some major problems go on for years. A loved one with a chronic or life-threatening illness is one such problem that comes to mind. This type of problem can leave you feeling exhausted and dispirited. Know that *living through* the problem is an achievement. Keep prompting yourself that you are truly amazing (because you are!)

Also, remind yourself of all the smaller problems that exist as a by-product of the major problem, and *how many of these you have overcome.*

Without doubt, overcoming far reaching, complex or major problems is challenging. *But...when you apply the 8 steps, in partnership with the knowledge, skills and attitudes presented in the following chapters of this book, you will be able to overcome the most complex of problems with strategy, skill and self-assurance!*

Chapter 4

A Practical Approach

Making time for the problem solving process

"Much may be done in those little shreds and patches of time which every day produces, and which most men throw away."

Charles Caleb Colton (English Writer, 1780-1832)

Unfortunately, your problems w*on't solve themselves* because you are reading this book.

Nor will they solve themselves if you write down the **'ACT TODAY'** acronym and display it in your study, office or work area. Putting the acronym in your desk, drawer, bag or briefcase won't work either.

Your problems won't even overcome themselves if you tattoo the *8 steps to overcoming problems* on your forehead. (Please don't try this!)

You must in fact, *make the time to execute* the problem solving steps, one-by-one.

Where are you supposed to find this time?

There are only twenty four hours in a day and seven days in a week and I'm assuming all your time is accounted for.

Therefore…you will need to *re-allocate* some of your time to schedule in 'problem solving time'.

At first this might seem absurd. I assure you that it isn't. You schedule in time for everything else, why not problem solving? It is one of the most crucial procedures in your life. How can you expect it to happen effectively if you don't devote any time to it?

What area/s of your life can you re-allocate time? As every area of your life is time poor, you can't possibly see where you can 'steal' some time. With your current mindset that seems true enough, but with an *altered mindset*, new possibilities appear.

Use the **'ACT TODAY'** acronym to solve the following problem.
"How can I create time to overcome my problems using the *8 steps*?"
To get you started here are some possible solutions to create blocks of time:

- watch less T.V.
- get up an hour earlier in the morning one or more days a week
- stay up an hour later one night a week
- cut down your technology/screen time (computer games, play station, social networking, texting etc).

During the thinking phase of the *8 steps* I'm sure you'll think of many more possible solutions.

Then, it's a matter of deciding which solution stands out and how and when to apply that solution. Once you've put your solution into action, you must of course review it – *check that you now have time to overcome your problems!*

Your reward can be whatever you choose, but your intrinsic reward is obvious... reclaiming time to actively overcome your problems whilst feeling empowered in the process!

The other time you can capture to work through the problem solving process, is the scattered segments of time each day produces. These are often times of *waiting.* If you train yourself to be aware of these opportunities, you will be amazed at their frequency and fruitfulness. I find these portions of time invaluable. Organise yourself to carry a pen and paper or a dictaphone to make a note of your thoughts and decisions.

Some such examples of time are:

- waiting at the traffic lights
- waiting for the lift
- waiting in a queue
- waiting for/travelling on public transport
- waiting for an appointment
- waiting for a friend/colleague
- waiting for a meeting
- waiting for children at school pick up/children's activities or sports.

Once you try it, you will never curse waiting time again!

Make today the day that *you find time* in your life for the problem solving process.

One problem at a time

"One thing at a time, all things in succession. That which grows fast withers as rapidly; and that which grows slow endures."

Josiah Gilbert Holland (American Novelist, 1819-1881)

Do you ever feel as though *every single thing* in your life is a problem? Whichever way you turn, there's another one. If you take the time to write down all these problems, you will probably find that many of them are related. That's a good thing, because it means you really don't have hundreds of problems to overcome. You just have some bigger problems made up of smaller problems. If your problems are not related, that's fine too, as long as you identify them.

It is important to realise that you can only deal effectively with one problem at a time. Prioritise your problems in order of importance or urgency. If you are having difficulty with this, pick one main problem out of those you have identified and use it as your starting point.

Now that you have your problems recorded, you can stop the chaos in your head. With a one-by-one problem solving strategy, your thoughts will regain clarity.

Put the problem in perspective

"What is true by lamplight is not always true by sunlight."
Joseph Joubert (French Writer, 1754-1824)

It's imperative that you put your problems in perspective otherwise they will consume you and your life. Do not let your problems define who you are.

➤ Remember, you are not the problem, your whole life is not the problem and all is not a disaster. You may *feel* this way at the time, but be aware that it's just not true. The problem is *one element* of your life; put it in perspective and keep it there. Make use of the word 'and' in your self-talk. For example, I have a son who is not getting better from his illness *and* I am a great employee, tennis player and mum/dad.

➤ Set boundaries for yourself in terms of the time you spend thinking about/working on the problem. Don't let it consume all your time and energy. Balance is important or you will experience 'burnout'.

➤ Do not talk incessantly about your problem. Talk about something else. Anything else.

➤ Do not identify yourself in terms of the problem. Identify yourself as you. What are you good at? What are you reading/watching/learning/doing/enjoying at the moment?

➤ You may find it helpful to visualise boxes in your mind. Your mind stores lots of boxes with lots of different subject labels. If a problem is consuming you, create a new mental box and label it 'problem'. Now open the lid and put the problem inside the box. Close the lid and know that the problem is safely stored until you choose to access it.

➤ Learn to remain calm in the midst of a problem. Panic lets your problem hold you to ransom.

Ask yourself some quality questions to help put the problem in perspective from a 'big picture' viewpoint.

1. How will this problem affect me one year from now?

2. How will this problem affect me five years from now?

3. What is the worst case 'scenario' for this problem?

Always remind yourself to put your problems in perspective and to *keep them there*!

Learning styles

"You have your way. I have my way. As for the right way, the correct way, and the only way, it does not exist."

Friedrich Nietzsche (German Philosopher, 1844-1900)

As you now know, the *8 steps to overcoming problems* is a series of steps or stages to keep you on track and ensure that you engage in a thorough problem solving process.

That said, the way in which you problem-solve, within this framework, can be as individual as you are.

There isn't an all-purpose best style, but there will be a best style for you.

Like most people, you probably use a combination of communication methods and learning styles, but you are likely to have one preferred method or style. This will be a relative strength for you. Figure out your preferred learning style and apply it in a practical way when you are doing the work in each problem solving step.

- If you favour a *visual* style, you will find it helpful to write things down or draw images or diagrams. *Seeing* your ideas on paper or on a screen is the best way for you to process information.
- If you favour a *kinaesthetic* style, you will find it helpful to imagine how your ideas/options/decisions would make you *feel* if you experienced them. Imagining 'the doing' of your options or choices is the best way for you to process information.
- If you favour an *auditory* style, you will find it helpful to hear your ideas/options/decisions as the spoken word. Hearing your choices spoken aloud by either yourself or someone else is the best way for you to process information.

Take advantage of your natural learning style/s so you can perform the *8 problem solving steps* as easily as possible.

Practice makes perfect

"Practice is the best of all instructors"
Publilius Syrus (Roman Writer, 85-43 B.C.)

As with most things in life, the more often you do something, the more efficient and effective you become at doing it. Ideally, you will find that problems become faster and easier to overcome the more you use the *8 steps*. With practice:

- ➤ your awareness of problems will become sharper
- ➤ you will be able to clarify problems accurately and succinctly
- ➤ you will become skilled at asking quality questions
- ➤ you will think of possible solutions more quickly, creatively and productively
- ➤ identifying the best solution will become faster and easier
- ➤ you will decide how and when to apply your solution assuredly
- ➤ you will put your solution into action and review that action with confidence
- ➤ you will enjoy your reward deservingly.

With practice, you can pave the way to your blockbuster life.

Chapter 5

Lessons to Learn

Thoughts – Feelings – Actions

"Thought is the parent of the deed."

Thomas Carlyle (Scottish Philosopher, 1795-1881)

What you think about, what you feel about, is what you bring about. In other words, *thoughts drive feelings which drive actions.*

➤ Thoughts are things! They can be changed and directed.

➤ Do you realise that *you can control your thoughts?*

➤ Your thoughts are *the* most important thing for you to monitor and manage because they ultimately determine what action you take or don't take in problem solving.

➤ *Your thoughts create your emotions,* not the other way around.

➤ What you think about and how you think about it, leads to what you feel and how you feel about it.

➤ Your emotional state then drives your actions and behaviours.

➤ So how you feel determines what you do and how you do it.

Try 'stepping outside your mind' and becoming *aware* of your thoughts. Observe them. Listen to them. Sit with them. Practise this often. As you notice your thoughts, ask yourself whether they serve you well. Ask yourself if you would benefit by changing them. Ask yourself whether you are *controlling your thoughts* or whether your thoughts are controlling you. Ascertain what changes you need to make so you are:

➤ *aware* of your thoughts

➤ *controlling* your thoughts

➤ *monitoring* and *reviewing* your thoughts to ensure they are supporting your problem solving abilities.

Never underestimate the power of thought.

Mindset

"Men are disturbed not by things, but by the view which they take of them."
Epictetus (Greek Philosopher, 55-135)

Your mindset is made up of your fixed mental attitudes, thoughts, responses and interpretations towards situations.

The way you see and deal with your problems is largely determined by your mindset.

Discover your current mindset using the following questions.
- Are you problem obsessed or solution focused?
- Do you find the positives in a situation or the negatives?
- Do you think things through from an optimistic angle or a pessimistic angle?
- Is your glass half full or half empty?
- Are you the victim or the victor of your problems?
- Do you choose your attitude to the day's events or do you let the day's events choose your attitude?
- Do you greet each day full of hope and vigour or curse all the problems the day might bring?

- Do you 'act on' or 'react to' problems?
- Are you proactive in your approach to problem solving?
- Do you wait for opportunities to come along or do you create your own opportunities?
- Do you do what's easy or do what works when it comes to overcoming problems?
- Do you have a 'can do' or a 'can't do' attitude?

Your mind is largely your reality. Take charge of it.

Will problem solving be easier if you give your mind a spring clean?

Will problem solving be easier if you choose to see your world, your life and your problems through a different lens?

You will be able to see *beyond limitations* if you alter your mindset and search for possibilities, rather than stifling your attitudes, thoughts, reactions and interpretations with finite boundaries or limits.

To alter your mindset you must *train yourself* to pause before you speak and act. This pause time is your opportunity to do 3 things.

1. Become aware of your current or habitual mindset *right now.*
2. Examine this mindset and decide whether you wish to maintain it, or change it.
3. Do the mental work to change your mindset *before offering your reply.*

I refer to this process as '*pressing my pause button*'. I remind myself to press my pause button often. Sometimes I may be halfway through a sentence and I hear myself saying things that are negative. I realise that I haven't pressed my pause button…so I stop what I'm saying or doing and re-wind the situation. I begin again, this time pressing my pause button first, so I can examine and adjust my mindset if necessary.

Training yourself to *press your pause button* takes time and practice. It's an *ongoing* exercise, but one that I highly recommend.

A word of warning – beware of changing your mindset to one of perfection. Perfection is a construct that does not exist. You will be disappointed every time. Instead, strive for a *positive improvement* in your mindset.

Over time, you will find that choosing a positive mindset is both achievable, and influential in your ability to better problem-solve!

Self-talk

"If you hear a voice within you saying, "You are not a painter," then by all means paint… and that voice will be silenced."

Vincent Van Gogh (Dutch Artist, 1853-1890)

As you go about your daily life you are constantly thinking about and interpreting your experiences. It's as though you have an internal voice inside your head giving opinions and suggestions about your life. It asks questions, makes statements and offers judgements about how you are managing your reality. At times it chats away at you incessantly. This inner voice is called your self-talk and it includes your conscious thoughts as well as your unconscious beliefs.

Your self-talk can be either positive or negative.

Negative self-talk is:

➤ a total waste of time and energy
➤ an adverse mental and emotional pastime
➤ a habit that digs you a deeper and deeper hole of inadequacy and self-loathing that becomes increasingly difficult to eliminate.

Let's be honest. How can you overcome problems when your self-talk habitually consists of telling yourself you are hopeless, dumb, an idiot and you can't do anything right? If you tell yourself often enough that you can't do something, then you *can't*. Your thoughts become your reality.

Positive self-talk is:

➤ a great investment of your time and energy

➤ a mental and emotional strategy that helps you overcome problems

➤ a tool that increases your ability to think, feel and act to the best of your ability.

When you habitually tell yourself you are amazing, wise and proactive, then you have a much better chance of being those things. Those traits help you solve problems. If you tell yourself often enough that you can do something, then you *can*. Your thoughts become your reality.

The good news is that *you* are in charge of your self-talk. It's your brain, your mind and your thoughts.

You alone have the capacity to change your self-talk from negative to positive.

Firstly, you must learn to tune in to your self-talk.

➤ Be aware of what that voice inside your head is telling you.
➤ Listen in regularly.
➤ What messages are you telling yourself over and over again?
➤ Are the messages draining or encouraging?

Understand that once you learn how to tune in to your self-talk, it becomes a powerful tool that can be used to your advantage. It's like changing a radio station. If you don't like the song, change the station. Learn to change the station on your self-talk as regularly as necessary until you find the positive talk back radio show. Using the comments in the table opposite, conduct your own self-talk appraisal.

➤ Ask yourself which comments sound familiar.
➤ Ask yourself which comments will help you problem-solve effectively.
➤ Make the necessary adjustments to your self-talk so it can *support* you in overcoming problems.
➤ Commit to only tuning in to positive self-talk.
➤ I can't stress enough the importance of *substituting negative self-talk with positive self-talk.*

Pay attention to your self-talk; it can make or break you.

I can't do this	I can do this
It won't work	It will work
I hate myself	I like myself
I can't do anything right	I can do lots of things right
It's my fault	How can I best solve this problem?
Why is this happening to me?	What can I learn from this so it doesn't happen again?
What would I know?	I know lots of things
I can't deal with this	I have the strength to deal with this
This is too hard for me	What do I need right now to help me manage this situation?
I hate my life	My life is good
My life is over	My life is not over
What was I thinking?	Things will be O.K.
I'm such an idiot	I'm not an idiot
I'm hopeless	I'm hopeful

Reframing

"I always tried to turn every disaster into an opportunity."
John D. Rockefeller (American Businessman, 1839-1937)

When you're problem solving and you strike an obstacle, *do not give up.*

Be clear with yourself; you are not going to fail, you are not stopping and you are definitely not defeated. The situation simply calls for a *change in definition.*

This is called *reframing.*

Reframing involves taking your situation or obstacle and observing it from a different angle to create a positive mindset.

A new perspective or viewpoint leads to renewed thoughts, emotions and actions.

To kick start your reframe, try asking some quality questions.
- What are some other ways of looking at this situation?
- How can I see this situation in a more positive light?
- How can I state this situation in a different way?
- What is good about this situation?
- What can I learn from this situation?
- How can overcoming this situation assist me?

You will be able to think of other questions to start a reframe. Whatever puts you in a productive, positive mindset is what is required here. Try it. Practise it.

The minute my mind begins to talk in negatives, a voice inside my head speaks up and tells my mind to stop being so pessimistic. The voice then says, "This isn't helpful. How can you see this situation in a more positive light? What do you need to work on?"

When this happens I can literally hear my mind sighing with relief, and then I sense an emotional shift within myself from negative to positive, simply because I reframed.

The skill of reframing is incredibly useful. The more you use it, the more automatic it becomes.

Reframing in action

I'm at the supermarket buying ingredients for dinner. I've conditioned myself to write a shopping list and only buy the food that I have written down. I'm feeling hungry and as I wait at the checkout, I take a chocolate bar from the candy display. (Chocolate is not on my shopping list!) I give the chocolate bar to the cashier to scan, and then eat the whole bar as I load my groceries into the trolley. "What's wrong with you?" says the voice inside my head. "You're hopeless! I knew you were a fat pig."

The reframing voice inside my head quickly interrupts… "Hang on a minute. This kind of talk isn't helpful. Stop it. Think. How can I look at what just happened in a different way? O.K. A positive first – I have been going to the gym regularly and following a healthy diet. Well done.

But unfortunately I just ate a chocolate bar that I shouldn't have eaten. Not so well done. Why did I eat that chocolate bar in the first place? I guess I was hungry and it happened to be there. Not a great weight management decision I'll admit, but instead of beating up on myself for something that I can't change, I'm going to ask myself what I can learn from this situation so it doesn't happen again.

O.K. So what can I learn?

For a start, I'm not going to go to the supermarket when I'm hungry. And if I do need to shop when I'm hungry, I'll grab a piece of fruit, and have it ready in my hand before I reach the checkout. And if I still can't trust myself, I'll go to the confectionary free checkout! Great thinking. Make sure I do it!"

Emotional intelligence

"Always be mindful of the kindness and not the faults of others."
Buddha (Leader, 563-483 B.C.)

Emotional intelligence is a modern day concept. Some people believe it is a better predictor of life success than Intelligence Quotient (I.Q.). As human beings we are emotional, interactive creatures so our emotional intelligence is an extremely relevant and useful ability to develop and use.

If you can determine, identify, manage, re-direct and choose your emotional responses to people and situations, you have a high level of emotional intelligence. If you can demonstrate empathy and self-control and an ability to emotionally connect with others, you have a high level of emotional intelligence. You can see how emotional intelligence is an asset when problem solving.

I find it staggering to think that until recent times, emotional intelligence had been largely unrecognised, under-valued and under-estimated.

But things are changing…

My thirteen year old daughter was nominated for class captain at school yesterday. She had to write her candidate speech last night. As she practised her speech delivery, it struck me that her entire presentation revolved

around her emotional intelligence and the value this could bring to her class. There was no mention of her academic ability, sporting prowess, musical talent, (great mum!!) or the fact that she loves animals.

It was all based around her ability to have a working awareness of her thoughts, feelings and actions and how she can put this intelligence into practice. She explained how her own awareness, leads her to an awareness of her peers' thoughts, feelings and actions, enabling her to support and guide her peers on an emotional level.

Emotional intelligence plays a significant role in the quality of your personal interactions with both yourself and others.

A high level of emotional intelligence enables your rational mind to guide and direct emotional thought processes so that they don't cloud interpretations, judgements and decisions.

It's important to realise that your emotional intelligence can be increased at any time.

Take a moment to reflect on your current level of emotional intelligence and ask yourself if it is helping or hindering your ability to overcome problems. The answer to this question will create that all important *awareness* that is necessary to bring about change.

Change

"Things do not change; we change."

Henry David Thoreau (American Writer, 1817-1862)

Problem solving is about finding solutions, not attempting to control situations or change people. You must work out *what you can change* and *let go* of what you can't.

Here are the things you can change regarding problem solving.

- ➤ Your thoughts, feelings and actions.
- ➤ The process you use to solve problems.
- ➤ Your mindset about problems.
- ➤ Your attitude towards problem solving.
- ➤ Your self-talk about your problem solving ability.
- ➤ Your level of emotional intelligence.
- ➤ The outcomes you achieve.

Here are the things you cannot change regarding problem solving.

- ➤ *Anything at all about how another person thinks, feels, talks or acts.*

You can:

- advise
- encourage
- educate
- lead
- model
- set an example
- counsel

- direct
- recommend
- inform
- suggest
- guide
- support
- instruct.

But you cannot change another person. Ever. You can only change yourself.

This is a very important, very relevant life lesson, but one that can take some people a lifetime to learn. If your problem solving strategy includes waiting for another person/people to change, be warned – you may be in for a very long wait!

To improve your problem solving ability, give your attention to the things that *you can change.*

Right or wrong

"There is nothing either good or bad, but thinking makes it so."
William Shakespeare (From the Play 'Hamlet') (English Dramatist, 1564- 1616)

There is no right or wrong in solving problems, only *what you think* is right or wrong.

Like most things, right and wrong are open to your *personal interpretation.* The right approach to solving a problem for you may well be the wrong approach to solving the same problem for another person. Take note; you are both right, as 'right' and 'wrong' are the products of personal, contextual thought. Possible solutions are not right or wrong until *your thoughts label them* as such. Up until that point they are just possible solutions. Your thinking makes them the right solution or the wrong solution, once you choose one and discard the others.

Trust that whatever decision you make is the right one at any given point in time. That's all you can ask of yourself and that's all anyone can ask of you.

Down the track, try not to look back and criticise yourself. *Hindsight* can be misleading. It will sing your praises if you make a winning choice or it will shoot you down in flames if your problem could have been solved more efficiently, less painfully or in a much shorter timeframe. This can be negative and self-destructive. Remind yourself that you are not a fortune teller and you cannot predict the future.

If you wish to learn from your problem solving experience, use hindsight to *reflect* upon it with curiosity, and *notice* what to do or what not to do next time should a similar problem arise.

When you choose that different 'right solution' next time, you will be demonstrating your newfound knowledge.

Advice

"I owe my success to having listened respectfully to the very best advice, and then going away and doing the exact opposite."

Gilbert K. Chesterton (English Writer, 1874-1936)

Advice is simply that, advice. You can take it or leave it, depending on whether it fits your situation advantageously. Only you know what it is like to walk in your shoes, and only you know your situation firsthand.

Be prepared to receive unwanted advice from some people. They think they are helping. Thank them politely and stay calm and focused.

At times you may actively seek out advice from certain people. Once again, thank them for their time and thoughts. Filter out what was beneficial to you and what wasn't. Just because you asked for advice, does not mean you must take it. That's the beauty of advice! Ideally, advice is a means of generating options.

Don't confuse seeking advice with seeking approval. Seeking approval involves dependence, seeking advice involves exploring ideas.

In the end, be sure that *you* decide your course of action. It's your problem and you are accountable for the outcome.

Acceptance as a solution

"We cannot conquer fate and necessity, yet we can yield to them in such a manner as to be greater than if we could."

Walter Savage Landor (English Poet, 1775-1864)

Some things in life just are, and there's nothing you can do about them, but accept.

Sometimes there isn't a solution to a problem apart from acceptance. You can't change what you can't change. But you can change your *thinking*. Acceptance under these circumstances can be liberating.

True acceptance is an inner acceptance of *what is*. It does not mean that you've given up hope; it does mean that you've come to the realisation that overcoming this problem is beyond you or anyone else's human capabilities right now. This type of solution takes strength and courage. (I know. I've been there.)

It may be that a problem needs to be accepted until it is outlived. So the solution for right now is, *'this is how it is, but things will change in time'*.

Acceptance is not a way of solving problems if it's by default. It needs to be *chosen* as your solution. It often becomes the solution to a problem when every other possible solution has been consciously explored to no avail. Under such circumstances, acceptance can be a truly wonderful discovery.

Recognise that sometimes you may *think* you've accepted a situation and yet you feel bitter. Such bitterness is an example of *inner resistance* to your solution. You are fighting your decision of acceptance. This inner resistance signals your need to re-visit the problem and re-visit your solution. You need to *review* and take *further action.*

Depending on the problem, remember to consider acceptance as a possible solution to your problem, during the thinking phase of the *8 steps.*

Reflection

"I love the man that can smile in trouble, that can gather strength from distress, and grow brave by reflection."

Thomas Paine (English Writer, 1737-1809)

You can glean valuable information from your problem solving experiences when you reflect upon them.

Reflection involves having a closer look at a situation with interest.

Reflection can highlight what to do next time and what not to do.

Reflection involves asking yourself some quality questions.

- What worked well here and why?
- What didn't work so well and why not?
- What would I do differently if given the same situation over again?
- What can I learn from this experience?
- What can I see now that I couldn't see when I was solving the problem?

Pay attention to your answers. They provide you with insight.

Where there are lessons, learn from them and move on graciously. Do not engage in blame or negative self-talk. Be grateful for the learning opportunity and promise yourself to apply your new wisdom.

Remember, experience cannot be bought or sold. Treat it with respect.

When it comes to overcoming problems, reflection is an under-utilised, invaluable skill waiting for you to reap its benefits.

Be open to new ways

"Presumption must be quenched even more than a fire."
Heraclitus (Greek philosopher, 540–480 B.C.)

Recognise that at times, your problem solving technique benefits from a fresh approach.

Challenge yourself, break the mould or deviate from your current way of thinking. When you are open to new ways of thinking, feeling and doing, you are open to continuous learning. This can only support your problem solving abilities.

Never presume you know it all. There is *always* more to learn.

You may already be an expert at overcoming problems and if so, you deserve congratulating. Well done.

But your current way of problem solving may not necessarily be the right way or the best way, for the rest of your life.

Imagine if there was another way, a different way, a more productive way, a more satisfying way of overcoming problems and you missed it because you thought you already knew everything.

No matter what your current state of expertise, always be open to new ways. At the very least with the onset of a new challenge, aim for skill refinement.

When you are open to new ways of thinking and doing, 3 outcomes are likely.

1. Your problem solving skills become dynamic, rather than one-dimensional or non-negotiable.
2. You embrace change which leads to learning, growth, new perspectives and opportunity.
3. Your problem solving skills evolve.

Flexibility in thinking is empowering!

Chapter 6

Behaviours and Emotional States to Embrace

Align with your core values

"Two things fill the mind with ever new and increasing wonder and awe, the more often and the more seriously reflection concentrates upon them: the starry heaven above me and the moral law within me."

Immanuel Kant (German Philosopher, 1724-1804)

When you problem-solve, it makes sense to choose a solution that aligns with your core values. Reason being, the likelihood of your problem being solved effectively will be much higher if your solution *matches* your core values, enabling you to sit comfortably with it.

As an example, let's imagine that Rachel is not getting along very well with her friend Meg. They are hardly speaking and Rachel knows it's because of something that happened last weekend.

Rachel decides to follow the *8 steps to overcoming problems* as follows.

1. Rachel is *aware* of the problem and *admits* to herself that she has a problem with Meg.

2. Rachel *clarifies* the problem.

3. Rachel *asks quality questions* about how to best overcome it.

4. She records answers to these questions as possible solutions during the *thinking phase.*

5. Rachel evaluates her possible solutions and chooses the solution that *stands out...* 'telling Meg a lie about what happened last weekend'.

6. Rachel makes some *decisions* about *how* and *when* to lie. She arranges a time and place to meet with Meg.

7. When they meet, Rachel puts her solution into *action... she lies to Meg.* Rachel *reviews* the outcome of her action shortly after. The outcome is great because her problem is solved. Rachel knows this because she and Meg are talking again and getting along well.

8. Rachel searches for the positive feelings associated with her actions *but they are not there.* She doesn't feel proud and wonderful. She feels the opposite. *Why is this?*

It's because Rachel solved the problem *out of alignment* with one of her core values; the value of honesty. Rachel is not going to be able to have a quality relationship with Meg for much longer – she is feeling guilty and uncomfortable around Meg. Rachel's problem is solved on the outside, but *not on the inside.*

9. Rachel reviews the outcome of her action again, and realises that she has not solved the problem effectively at all. There is a discrepancy between her solution of telling Meg a lie and her core value of honesty. Rachel needs to take further action. *Rachel goes back to step 5* and *re-evaluates* her possible solutions. This time she chooses a solution that is *in alignment with her value of honesty* as well as her other core values!

It is clearly beneficial to know your core values, so you can cross reference them with your possible solutions.

➤ What are *your* core values or principles?

➤ Are you *familiar* with them?

Here are some values to get you thinking:

achievement	friendship	physical challenge
advancement	making a difference	knowledge/learning
fame	fun	power and authority
adventure	health	promotion
privacy	family	the arts
helping others	public service	co-operation
change	creativity	honesty
close relationships	inner peace	independence
security	community	positivity
competence	commitment	excellence
country	loyalty	financial gain
freedom	stability	security
status	leadership	working alone
money	self-respect	working with others
personal development	love	ecological awareness

Record *your values* so you can refer to them when you are overcoming problems.

Self-belief

"Self-confidence is the first requisite to great undertakings."
Samuel Johnson (English Writer, 1709-1784)

When you believe in yourself, you have a greater understanding of who you are and how you wish to respond to situations. When that situation involves solving a problem, self-belief supports you with:

- a positive mindset
- calculated risk taking
- confidence in decision making
- a sense of self beyond the problem
- being the victor, not the victim
- staying with the problem solving process
- minimising emotional reactions
- not taking the problem personally
- tolerating minor setbacks
- putting healthy boundaries around the problem
- silencing negative self-talk
- activating character strengths to support you
- being solution focused.

If your self-belief is wavering, or hovering at low levels, you need to increase it. Begin by looking at all the things you have ever achieved in your life. There will be many. You will need to write these achievements down. Or draw them. Or record them in a way that is meaningful to you.

Write/draw/record anything and everything from learning to walk and learning to talk to going to school, learning to read, write and draw, developing relationships, getting a job, raising a family, learning to drive, solving problems of any size, sorting a cluttered cupboard, desk or drawer, painting something, planting a garden, growing your own vegetables, achieving in sport/leisure/hobbies, reading a book from cover to cover, learning a song or a poem or another language, making something, helping others, time scheduling your days, planning activities, and so forth.

This list is important.

Nothing on this list is trivial. Do not allow your mind to tell you otherwise.

Your self-talk may want to tell you about all the things you didn't do well, about when you didn't succeed, and about when you didn't finish what you started. Tell yourself how great it is that these memories can remind you of the opportunities life provides for learning and growth.

Now, *return to focus on your successes.* Think back to when each listed achievement occurred. Take yourself back to that time and place in your mind's eye.

- ➤ Can you see yourself?
- ➤ Who else is with you?
- ➤ How do you feel?
- ➤ What is going on around you?

Re-live these experiences and emotions. Take them on board once again. Let them create or boost your self-belief by reminding you of what you can do.

Repeat this process of focusing on your past successes over and over again. Do it as long as it takes, as often as it takes, until you experience a shift in your level of self-belief.

You have achieved much in your life so far. Believe that you have much more potential to be explored. Jump up and down about yourself. Back yourself. The odds are looking good. Know that you are on the way to becoming a great problem solver and creating a blockbuster life.

Focus

"If I have ever made any valuable discoveries, it has been owing more to patient attention than to any other talent."

Sir Isaac Newton (English mathematician and physicist, 1642 - 1727)

What is focus?

> ➤ Focus is about concentration.
> ➤ It's about giving deliberate attention to the task at hand.
> ➤ It's about application.
> ➤ It's about doing what you need to do unwaveringly.

Why is focus important when problem solving?

> ➤ So your problem can be overcome the best way possible, whilst minimising negative consequences and maximising positive outcomes.

What can interrupt focus?

> ➤ Distractions.
> ➤ Procrastination.
> ➤ Boredom.
> ➤ Laziness.

> ➤ Loss of motivation.
> ➤ Poor time management.
> ➤ Lack of self-discipline.
> ➤ Feeling uncomfortable.

How can you stay focused in order to overcome your problems?

- Set yourself deadlines for each step of the **'ACT TODAY'** acronym.
- Make yourself accountable for your problem by telling someone. That way, they can check-in with you regularly and help to keep you on track.
- Keep a diary/notebook/folder of information about each step of the problem solving process.
- Plan/set aside/schedule in regular times when you problem-solve.
- Turn off your phone/divert your calls and put a 'meeting in progress' sign on your door.
- Find a problem solving buddy so you can bounce ideas around.
- Promise yourself a treat when you have accomplished a certain number of steps within the *8 steps*.
- Imagine the implications if you don't solve the problem. (A form of self-blackmail!)

Focus is vital when you are overcoming problems. It's a behaviour you can learn when you adapt your environment and refuse to succumb to any interruptions or distractions.

Zest, enthusiasm and energy

"Cheerfulness gives elasticity to the spirit."
Samuel Smiles (Scottish Writer, 1812-1904)

You will discover that these three emotional states or character strengths are indispensable, when it comes to seeing the problem solving process through from start to finish.

If you have to overcome a problem, you will get the best results with a great attitude.

Just the words themselves…

➤ zest

➤ enthusiasm

➤ energy

…create a feeling of positivity.

Add in the following words to boost your problem solving mindset even further:

vigour	liveliness	power
keenness	gusto	get-up-and-go
passion	eagerness	interest
strength	zeal	excitement
intensity	commitment	dedication

When you tackle a problem 'full on' with a 'can do' attitude, the process of solving it can be enjoyable and uplifting. You feed off your own energy and enthusiasm until overcoming your problem becomes an exhilarating experience. This type of momentum takes time and practice to build, but it is attainable!

Determination/persistence/willpower

"Nothing in the world can take the place of persistence. Talent will not; nothing is more common than unsuccessful people with talent. Genius will not; unrewarded genius is almost a proverb. Education will not; the world is full of educated derelicts. Persistence and determination alone are omnipotent. The slogan "press on" has solved and always will solve the problems of the human race."

Calvin Coolidge (American 30th President of the United States, 1872-1933)

When problem solving gets tough and a solution feels beyond reach, determination, persistence and willpower become invaluable.

There are countless times, when overcoming my children's complex health and medical problems, I've had to dig deeper and deeper, only to discover there was nothing left to dig for.

In these times, it was sheer determination, persistence and willpower that got me over the line.

One of the things that kept me going was the knowledge that these were my children and that nobody else was prepared to overcome their health problems with my same level of commitment. It was up to *me* to be proactive. It was up to *me* to go in to bat for their problems.

Not even a comment from a highly trained medical specialist about my son's deteriorating health could dampen my determination, persistence and willpower. I remember the words clearly because they rang in my ears from that day on for years to come – "Sometimes in medicine you have to say I don't know. This is one of those times. I'm sorry."

I went home, with the awareness and admission that I now had a more serious problem. I also went home with a further increase in my determination level!

I sat in my study, clarified the problem, asked some more quality questions then began the thinking phase. At first my page was blank and remained so for quite some time. The thinking phase was painfully difficult and I drew upon all the resources available to me.

I thought, I asked questions and I researched. I became extremely proficient on the internet. I read medical article after medical article and medical journal paper after medical journal paper. I found most of the content extremely challenging to understand initially, because of the unfamiliar terminology. But I persisted with a medical dictionary.

I called on my logic and my intuition, my past knowledge and experience; I called on anything and everything.

I broke through all pre-conceived limitations and barriers. Nothing seemed unreasonable.

I communicated with medical specialists overseas, I discovered tests for things I didn't know existed and I insisted on having all my theories explored.

In my research, I discovered somebody who believed they had an answer to my son's problem of ill health. A treatment pathway was presented and with further investigation and a massive dose of hope, I made a decision to act. On review, it was clear that the problem had been solved. My unwell son had regained his health, via what appeared to be a miracle!

For so long I referred to my son's recovery as a miracle... until one day somebody said to me... "Sally, your son did not recover because of a miracle, he recovered because of your absolute *determination, persistence* and *willpower!!*"

Character strengths

"He who is plenteously provided for from within needs but little from without."
Johann Wolfgang Goethe (German Poet, 1749-1832)

Character strengths are *internal resources.* They are attributes assigned to you because you are human.

You may not be aware of all the character strengths you can access. It's quite an impressive collection.

The nature of the problem you are overcoming will determine which character strengths you need to activate.

Every single time you have a problem to solve, pick what you need from your *catalogue of character strengths* and put it to work for you. This may appear a very strange concept, especially if you are unfamiliar with how your character strengths can support you in overcoming problems. Try it out regardless.

Here are some of the character strengths available to you in the catalogue of human strengths. You may think of others.

honesty	hope	humility
caution	love	courage
commitment	gratitude	self-control
creativity	joy	teamwork
forgiveness	kindness	curiosity
empathy	wisdom	patience
enthusiasm	playfulness	perseverance
critical thinking	fairness	leadership
perspective	self-knowledge	spirituality

Start with one or two strengths at a time. Write them out on cards and display them on your desk, on the fridge or on your bedside table, for example. Read or say them *often. Internalise* them. Imagine or visualise how these strengths will support you in overcoming your problem. Then let these strengths *guide you* in all *8 steps* of the problem solving process.

Hope

"A leader is a dealer in hope."

Napolean Bonaparte (French Leader, 1769-1821)

Overcoming complex, major problems is often a journey of ups and downs.

Hope is what you can draw upon when all seems hopeless.

In your darkest day, hope is what brings the promise of a fresh tomorrow.

When problem solving is interwoven with hope, your positive mindset can be kept alive.

I can recall numerous times when I've had to force myself to rely on hope when there was little else left to grasp.

Without hope, I would not have overcome many challenging problems; problems where no one had walked before.

Without hope, I would not have created many unique solutions; solutions that nobody had dreamt before.

Hope has played a large role in making me the problem solver that I am today.

When you have hope, anything is possible.

Courage

"Whatever you do, or dream you can, begin it. Boldness has genius and power and magic in it."

Johann Wolfgang Goethe (German Poet, 1749-1832)

The great Greek philosopher Socrates described courage as "intelligent endurance". I find this definition useful when deciding if my problem solving strategy is courageous or foolish.

➤ Courage is what shows up when problem solving gets tough.

➤ Courage is when you want to run and hide from your problems, but instead you stay with them, finding strength, even if you have to borrow it.

➤ Courage is going beyond what you thought were your capabilities, in order to overcome a problem.

➤ Courage is asking, "What do I need to do now?" over and over again, even when you're all out of answers. Courage is creating those answers.

➤ Courage is daring to go where you have not been, so a resolution can be achieved.

➤ Courage is asking the bold questions, choosing the bold options, making the bold decisions and taking the bold actions to see a problem through.

➤ Courage is never taking no for an answer, until *you decide* no is the answer.

Courage is a prerequisite for a blockbuster life. It enables you to achieve outcomes that you once thought were out of reach.

Apologising

"Right actions in the future are the best apologies for bad actions in the past."
Tryon Edwards (American Theologian, 1809-1894)

In certain contexts, an apology may be just what's required to overcome a problem.

The good news is that apologising is a small act relative to its potential outcome. To offer an apology, look at the person you are apologising to and say with sincerity, *"I am sorry to have hurt you."* This genuine gesture can work wonders. If you've tried it you will know.

For your apology to truly hold weight, *a change in your behaviour* must accompany it. That's the lesson in an apology – it highlights the need to do something *different.* Demonstrate this difference or your apology becomes null and void.

I am staggered by the number of people who find it almost impossible to offer an apology. Why is this so?

➤ An apology is not about you, it's about something *you said* or *didn't say* or *did* or *didn't do.*

➤ An apology does not make you inferior or incompetent. Rather, it's a sign of humility and respect, for yourself and others.

➤ An apology costs nothing but its effect can be priceless, for both you and the recipient.

➤ An apology is a powerful tool to have in your problem solving toolkit.

Take some time now to reflect on whether you owe anybody an apology.

Apologies of a different kind may be required when a breakdown in communication occurs. Communication breakdowns are inevitable in relationships. If someone *misinterprets* your look, action or comment, a brief, simple apology can short circuit a potential problem.

I know and you know that you didn't *intentionally* plan to hurt anyone, but an apology such as, "I am sorry that you are upset," acknowledges another person's feelings without laying blame.

Patience

"Have patience. All things are difficult before they become easy."
Saadi (Iranian Poet, 1184-1283)

Problem solving can take time. Remember, it's a process. Be patient with *yourself, others* and *the situation.*

Note that there is a big difference between procrastination and patience. Patience asks you to demonstrate endurance or staying power as well as tolerance. Patience requires you to remain focused without complaint, whilst waiting on the outcome of a process that you have set in motion. You may be waiting for information, for input, for resources or to hear back from somebody. Whatever it is, trust that you are doing all that you can at that moment and retain your composure.

I know this can be an extremely difficult thing to do, particularly when your problem feels urgent. But becoming anxious about things *beyond your control* will not be helpful. Instead it will encourage irritation, annoyance, intolerance and impulsivity.

Practise being still. Practise serenity. Know that I'm still learning this with you.

Humour

"Humor is the great thing, the saving thing. The minute it crops up, all our irritations and resentments slip away and a sunny spirit takes their place."

Mark Twain (American Writer, 1835-1910)

When overcoming problems, the serious side of your personality can take over. That's understandable, as problem solving calls for responsible, sensible, logic-based strategy.

However, remember to inject some light hearted humour into your day.

If you can't have a laugh at yourself or the situation, find an outlet that can provide you with some comic relief.

Here are some suggestions:
- watch a funny movie or TV show
- read a joke book
- check out the funny pages in the newspaper
- spend time with someone in your life who makes you laugh
- join your local 'laughter club'
- go to a comedy club.

Humour and laughter can be wonderful *respite* from the problem solving process, not to mention the *mental* and *physical health benefits* a good laugh can produce.

Laughter can do the following.

➤ Relax your whole body, relieving your physical tension and stress whilst re-booting your energy levels.

➤ Boost your immune system by decreasing stress hormones as well as increasing immune cells and infection-fighting antibodies.

➤ Trigger the release of endorphins which are a feel-good chemical produced by your body to give you a natural high.

➤ Protect your heart by improving blood vessel function and increasing blood flow.

➤ Disperse negative emotions. You can't feel worried, gloomy, or cross when you're laughing.

The expression 'laughter is the best medicine' offers wise advice. Laughter and its effects can have a significant positive influence on your problem solving capacity. So what are you waiting for? Get laughing!

Forgiveness

"Forgiveness does not change the past, but it does enlarge the future."

Paul Boese (Dutch Botanist, 1668-1738)

At times, what is required to overcome a problem is *forgiveness*.

Forgiveness is often a misunderstood act.

Forgiveness can be the pathway to *your* brighter future.

Forgiveness benefits *you*.

Forgiveness means both releasing the person/people who wronged you and being released from your story of pain.

By *releasing* and *letting go* of those who caused you hurt:

➤ you no longer need to hold onto resentment, injustice and thoughts of revenge

➤ you are free to be at *peace* with yourself and life

➤ you open the doorway to your *personal freedom*

➤ you activate growth and possibility in your life

➤ you can move into the present moment, leaving the past behind you, right where it belongs.

By *being released* you can:

➤ let go of the anger and angst you are harbouring

➤ stop repeating your painful, energy-sapping tale of woe over and over again

➤ use your energy for a productive and positive purpose

➤ end the destructive cycle of re-living your private grief 'day in, day out'.

Forgiveness allows you to *re-write your story*, so that painful thoughts and memories are neutralised and contextualised.

Forgiveness can be an extremely difficult process. I know. Be kind to yourself.

Forgiveness takes courage, strength of character and vision.

Have faith that your efforts will be well worth your reward.

Gratitude

"Gratitude is the fairest blossom which springs from the soul."
Henry Ward Beecher (American Clergyman, 1813-1887)

Adopt an attitude of gratitude in your life. Gratitude is a feeling of thankfulness or appreciation for things. It's free, and such an attitude can work wonders when you are struggling with life's problems.

Gratitude can turn a negative into a positive. It can uplift your mood and awaken your mind. Think of all the things you have to be thankful for and give thanks for them out loud. If you are struggling to think of things, begin with being thankful that you woke up this morning, that you have clean water to drink, a roof over your head and food to eat.

In my family we have reinterpreted the technological meaning of 'www'. For us, it stands for 'what went well'. 'www' is a game of gratitude that we often play at dinner time. As we are sitting around the table together, each person thinks of two things that went well for them throughout their day. One-by-one, we share these things with the rest of the family. During sharing time, we must state what aspect of these experiences we are grateful for and why. I find this gratitude game both therapeutic and balancing.

I am going to suggest that you learn to *express gratitude* for your problems. If you think this is a senseless idea, please hold back from your final judgement until you've tried it.

I'm proposing this for 3 reasons.

1. The first reason lies in the belief that your problems really do hold a valuable lesson or message within their solution. You can't buy this type of lesson. You can only experience it as you overcome a problem, particularly a far reaching, complex or major problem.

2. The second reason is that your problems can always be worse than they are. I know it does not *feel* that way when you are struggling with an extremely challenging situation that you need to overcome. In fact, I find there's nothing more exasperating than someone saying to you, "It could be worse you know" or "There's always someone worse off than you." These words are true, but I believe you need to be the one to realise them when you are ready. They will have an impact when they are formed in your own mind and come out of your own mouth, not from an unsolicited source with inappropriate timing.

3. The third reason is that overcoming problems is a means to personal growth. When you actively problem-solve, your capabilities develop and expand revealing your untapped potential. In short, you evolve as a person.

Aim to express gratitude for something in your life each and every day.

Chapter 7

Behaviours and Emotional States to Minimise

Stress

"In times of stress, be bold and valiant."

Horace (Roman Poet, 65-8 B.C.)

Stress is a physical, psychological and emotional response to changes or pressures in your environment or outside world. These changes or pressures are called *stressors.*

People, situations and events don't create stress. *You create stress* by interpreting these potential stressors as stressful.

You can notice stress by recognising the *physical, psychological* and *behavioural signs.*

Physical signs of stress are bodily changes or sensations you can *feel* in your body.

Your immediate reaction to a stressor is triggered by your brain. Your brain releases adrenalin which brings about these physical bodily changes such as:

➤ an increase in heart rate

➤ feeling anxious

➤ muscle tension

➤ a churning stomach

➤ sweating

➤ shaking.

Psychological signs of stress are *thoughts* or *feelings* of a specific nature such as:

➤ feeling overwhelmed

➤ being oversensitive to others' remarks

➤ being easily frustrated

➤ having thoughts of difficulty in coping/not coping.

Behavioural signs of stress are changes to the things that you *do* such as:

➤ an increase in alcohol consumption

➤ an increase in drug use

➤ over sleeping/under sleeping

➤ over eating/under eating

➤ a decrease in self-care – showering less frequently or wearing the same clothes for many days in a row for example

➤ procrastinating

➤ avoiding social contact

➤ having less outings and spending more time at home.

Your *vulnerability* to stressors is influenced by:

➤ genetics

➤ environment

➤ brain chemistry.

You can influence this vulnerability by adapting your environment whenever possible, recognising your stressors, recognising the signs and symptoms of stress and activating coping strategies.

Coping strategies are the skills/activities/behaviours you can use or activate to effectively reduce the negative effects of stressors and prevent stress from *accumulating*. A list of useful coping strategies includes:

- relaxation
- deep breathing
- meditation
- massage
- listening to music
- planning and organising
- structure and routine
- goal setting
- being assertive
- talking with your support people
- using a set of steps to problem-solve
- exercising
- healthy eating
- taking regular time out
- taking a stress management course.

If stress is allowed to *accumulate* it can negatively affect your mind and body. Accumulated stress can cause:

➤ lowered immunity
➤ illness/disease
➤ fatigue
➤ muscle aches
➤ headaches
➤ anxiety
➤ gastrointestinal disturbances
➤ mood disturbances
➤ concentration difficulties
➤ sleep disturbances
➤ appetite changes
➤ *difficulty problem solving*
➤ difficulty making decisions
➤ feelings of depression.

Stress affects your ability to problem-solve, so know your stressors, notice your stress signs and activate your coping strategies before stress has an opportunity to accumulate.

When you learn to *take notice* of your stress symptoms you will become better at *managing* your stress levels. You will be able to build resilience and protect yourself from the impact of your vulnerabilities and stressors.

It is important to mention that not all stress is negative. *Eustress* is a positive form of stress. It can be called *healthy stress* because it gives you *positive feelings* such as anticipation, excitement, pleasure and fulfilment. Eustress is stress that you have chosen or invited into your life.

Eustress is induced by positive or desirable life stressors such as:

- coming first in a race
- winning a job promotion
- watching a scary movie
- getting married
- having a baby
- riding a roller coaster
- taking a holiday
- *problem solving using a trusted set of steps with a positive outcome in mind.*

When you have an understanding of stress and stressors, you can make informed decisions about what your body is telling you and how best to manage those signs and symptoms.

Worry

"I have lived a long life and had many troubles, most of which never happened."
Mark Twain (American Writer, 1835-1910)

➤ What do you gain from worry?
➤ Does worry move you forward?
➤ Does worry help you solve problems?

Worry is a destructive habit. It leads to stress, which leads to headaches, anxiety, stomach pains and general ill health, which leads to more stress, and so the cycle repeats.

Worry is a *draining* emotion. Eliminate it from your life. Worry can be caused by *over thinking* your problem. Learn to quieten your mind.

1. Sit in a comfortable position and breathe.
2. Take slow deep breaths in, followed by slow deep breaths out.
3. This inhaling and exhaling will allow your mind and body an opportunity to expel some of the tension and worry they are carrying.
4. You can do this breathing exercise anytime, anywhere.
5. When you make it habitual, you can prevent worry from escalating.

A helpful strategy is to write down all your worries, then re-visit this worry list a short time later when you are not feeling as worried.

1. As you read through your worry list, see if you can examine each worry through the eyes of reality and probability.

2. Some of your worries will be about things that *have already happened.* Worry will not change them. Try to let go.

3. Some of your worries will be about things that *may or may not happen.* If they are within your control, stop worrying and start doing. If they are not within your control, once again, worry will not change them. Try to let go.

4. Some of your worries *will be created* by 'what if' type questions about things that may happen in the future. These are worries that you are creating in your imagination. They are not real. Try to use your thoughts more productively in the here and now.

When you cease worrying about your problems, you will have more energy to channel into solving them.

Anger

"Holding on to anger is like grasping a hot coal with the intent of throwing it at someone else; you are the one who gets burned."

Buddha (Leader, 563-483 B.C.)

It is OK to feel anger. Let your anger out safely. Let it pass. But if you *hold on* to anger, you are likely to become stuck in it. Long term anger is unhealthy.

The problem solving process can arouse frustration, which can then trigger *anger*. Anger is a *reactive* emotion. Things become dangerous when you allow your anger to short-circuit the problem solving work you have done to date, stopping you from solving your problem.

➤ Recognise when you feel anger.

➤ Learn to monitor your anger levels.

➤ Be aware of what triggers your anger.

➤ Write a list of your anger triggers and get to know this list intimately. That way you can circumnavigate anger episodes or at least put strategies in place to minimise them.

➤ Check in with how you are coping with anger management in the following areas.

  ➤ What are you thinking?
  ➤ What language are you using in your self-talk?
  ➤ What tone of voice are you using in your self-talk?
  ➤ Are you separating yourself from the problem or are you letting the problem control other areas of your life?
  ➤ Are you getting enough sleep?
  ➤ Are you eating regularly?
  ➤ Are you taking breaks to exercise/ pursue leisure activities?
  ➤ Are you in blame mode regarding this problem?
  ➤ Are you taking your anger out on others?
  ➤ Are you able to switch off from your anger?
  ➤ Are you stuck in self-pity because life is not fair?

Sometimes I feel so angry that I can barely think. I acknowledge my anger by saying out loud, "I feel angry!" Then I say, "This anger will pass. I need to give myself time. Is there anything I can do to make it pass faster?"

Activities where your mind and body are active and occupied can help release anger, such as:

- exercising
- sorting something such as a cupboard, a drawer, a filing cabinet or a shed
- cleaning something such as the car, the fridge, your tools or the windows
- mowing the lawn, gardening, grocery shopping, cooking/baking, making/building things.

I remember feeling extreme anger when I discovered my children's medical conditions had been wrongly diagnosed or incorrectly managed, and their health had suffered as a consequence. I experienced huge difficulties shaking this anger, until I learnt to ask myself *2 quality questions.*

1. How can I use my anger in a productive way?

2. How can I channel this negative energy into a positive outcome?

These two questions shifted my reactive response to the situation (anger) to an active response (thinking of possibilities). But that was just the first step. Next, these two questions shifted my active response, to a *proactive* response (creating positive change). This proactive response was the catalyst for the following outcomes.

➤ A multi-national company amending incorrect allergy information on their product packaging.

➤ Medical practitioners performing new procedures.

➤ The writing of children's books and articles to educate people about food allergies.

➤ The review of policy and procedure within the health sector.

➤ The establishment of education programs and professional development for clinicians which reflect best practice.

You need to remember that *anger is a reactive response to a trigger.* The problem solving process can be long and difficult so beware of triggers.

Use strategies so you can replace your *reactive* responses with *active* responses, or better still, *proactive* responses.

Guilt

"Guilt upon the conscience, like rust upon iron, both defiles and consumes it, gnawing and creeping into it, as that does which at last eats out the very heart and substance of the metal."

Bishop Robert South (English Theologian, 1634-1716)

Guilt is anger directed at yourself; at what you did or did not do. It is a 'red flag' that you have a problem to deal with.

Healthy guilt serves a purpose.

➤ It carries a legitimate lesson.

➤ It guides you to change your behaviour.

➤ It leads you to rectify something you said or did that was wrong.

➤ It prompts you to find a solution to a problem that is your responsibility.

Unhealthy guilt does not serve any rational purpose.

➤ It keeps you stuck in a pattern of self-directed negative emotions.

➤ It causes you prolonged anxiety.

➤ It propels your problem out of proportion.

➤ It paralyses your ability to take action.

When dealing with guilt use the following strategies.

1. Recognise your guilt for what it is – an emotional warning sign that something you said/did (didn't say/didn't do) needs attention.

2. Accept you have said/done something wrong or hurtful and that you cannot change the past.

3. Ask yourself what you said/did to cause your feeling of guilt.

4. Ask yourself what action you need to take to correct or repair the situation that's causing your guilt.

5. Take the necessary action to make amends and move on.

6. If you still feel guilty, ask if your guilt is rational or irrational.

7. If it's irrational, acknowledge this. Tell yourself that the guilt does not serve any purpose. Let it go.

8. If your guilt is rational ask yourself why you are *still* feeling guilty. Maybe you haven't fully learnt your lesson yet. Your guilt will remain or keep returning until you change your behaviour.

It is necessary to determine the cause of your guilt as soon as possible. Then you can take the action required to 'right your wrong', allowing your guilt to be released.

Fear

"Fear defeats more people than any other one thing in the world."
Ralph Waldo Emerson (American Poet, 1803-1882)

Fear is a basic survival mechanism. It's an emotional response to a *perceived threat*.

In problem solving, the perceived threat is your problem and/or the process of solving it. You may not like what you find when you 'unpack' the problem, you may be fearful of choosing the 'wrong' solution to overcome the problem or you may be afraid of acting on a solution because of the repercussions, for yourself and/or others.

When fear is identified, your instincts react to it in one of three ways – fight, flight or freeze.

1. A *fight response* is to take on your problem as the enemy, doing whatever it takes to defeat it.
2. A *flight response* is to flee or run away from your problem, not even attempting to solve it.
3. A *freeze response* is exactly that. You feel powerless to move your problem in any direction. So the problem remains exactly as it is and you feel stuck right where you are, unable to take any form of action.

In reality, you don't want to deal with your problem in any of these three ways, as they do not lead to an effective solution.

The key is having an *awareness* of your fear and having an *awareness* of your instinctive reaction to fear. Once you have this awareness, you can monitor your emotional reaction to a problem.

➤ When fear arises, note which response your body is telling you to take. Acknowledge that this is an instinctive response that is not relevant to the problem at hand. You are not a cave dweller needing to overcome a wild beast, as your ancestors did. You are in fact, living in the 21st Century.

➤ Instead of reacting to fear with a fight, flight or freeze instinct, you can recognise these feelings for what they are, and move yourself on towards the *8 steps to overcoming problems*, adopting a logical, rational approach to problem solving.

➤ Sometimes, despite a strategy, you will be left facing a scary problem or a decision that evokes fear in you. And you will be left to take action that scares you.

➤ Whatever your problem, whatever your solution and whatever the action is that you need to take, trust that you will be OK.

Sometimes you need to do what scares you in order to control your fear.

Feeling Overwhelmed

"The secret of getting ahead is getting started. The secret of getting started is breaking your complex overwhelming tasks into small manageable tasks, and then starting on the first one."

Mark Twain (American Writer, 1835-1910)

I know the feeling all too well. It feels like I'm struggling for breath. My head is spinning, my mind is racing and the world around me is a blur. Every noise sounds like a jackhammer.

I recognise what is happening to me. "It's OK," I tell myself, "You are feeling overwhelmed."

It is understandable that you may feel overwhelmed during the course of solving certain problems. Remember you are human. Even when you know all the theory of what to do and have put it into practice many times, you can still feel overwhelmed. Do not criticise yourself. Do not allow yourself to feel defeated. Instead, acknowledge that you feel overwhelmed and that you are going to do something about it. This alone should ease the feeling.

When you feel overwhelmed, ask yourself: "What do I need right now?"

Some ideas to get you thinking are:

- do something you enjoy
- watch a movie
- take a walk
- write down all your thoughts to get them out of your mind
- sleep
- exercise
- talk to a support person
- have a massage
- take a bath
- close your eyes and focus on your breathing
- listen to music
- punch a pillow
- sort your thoughts into problems and jot them down so you have clarity.

When time has passed and your mind has eased, acknowledge your problems, *one at a time.* Record them in some way; on paper in words or pictures, as diagrams, as an audio recording, on a screen or use whatever tool you prefer. Prioritise the problems or just pick one to solve first.

Follow the **'ACT TODAY'** acronym to overcome this problem.

'ACT TODAY'

1. **A**ware of and admit to having a problem

2. **C**larify the problem

3. **T**ime to ask quality questions

4. **T**he thinking phase

5. **O**ne solution stands out

6. **D**ecisions for your solution

7. **A**ct on and review your solution

8. **Y**our reward.

Then move onto solving your next problem, and after that, your next problem using the *8 steps*. If you feel overwhelmed again at any stage, (and you may) repeat the described procedure. Begin by asking yourself the same question as before, "What do I need right now?" Work out what it is you need and do/get/have/action it.

Everyone feels overwhelmed from time to time. It's how you *cope* with that feeling that is important.

Despair

"What we call despair is often only the painful eagerness of unfed hope."
George Eliot (English Novelist, 1819-1880)

Despair is such a wretched emotion to be trapped within. Especially when you know how to solve problems and you know how to find solutions. Sometime in your life you will strike a problem that's different from the rest. No matter how hard you try there appears to be no way out. There appears to be *no hope*, no future and no end in sight for you and your problem. Everything seems black and oh so gloomy. You are in despair!

Despair is ugly and all encompassing. It swallows you until you are unrecognisable to yourself. When a problem leads you to despair, you *must* find a glimmer of hope in something or someone. Ask for help. Keep asking for help. Despair is far too difficult to deal with on your own.

If family and friends cannot help you through your despair, and you continue in that emotional state, strongly consider making an appointment to see your local doctor and getting some professional help. It is very wise to seek help and support from trained professionals who are skilled in dealing with emotional problems like despair. They can assist you in finding a way through.

When you conquer your despair and resolve your problem, you will have built incredible resilience for whatever lies ahead. And when your despair is a thing of the past and you have forged ahead, remember to take a moment and look back in awe at what you overcame. Genuinely congratulate yourself.

Complaining

"To hear complaints is tiresome to the miserable and the happy."
Samuel Johnson (English Author, 1709-1784)

Complaining is a sign that you are not at peace with yourself or the world.

But complaining does not solve problems. Complaining *grows* problems. Complaining creates animosity and negativity.

Habitual complaining is toxic to both yourself and those around you.

If you have a problem, stop complaining about it and deal with it!

If you catch yourself complaining about someone or something, take note. Complaining is your signal that there is a problem to overcome. Complaining is a sign of resentment.

You need to stop seeing the problem as an enemy. View it as a problem that needs a solution.

Identify the problem and take action. If you can't find the problem, look harder. It will be there.

If you have already identified the problem, worked through the *8 steps* and your resolution was acceptance of the current situation, unfortunately you are not displaying this. You can't have embraced acceptance as a course of action if you are still complaining about the issue. Ask yourself why you are still resentful.

Complaining is not to be confused with *informing*. Informing a person/people about an error or deficiency so that it can be corrected and/or changed in the future, is not complaining if it is performed in a *non-blaming, non-personal, non-judgemental, factual* manner. This act can be very powerful for both the informer and the informant.

I 'inform' when I see a learning opportunity in problems that can make a difference to others. I find this experience both humbling and empowering.

Procrastination

"Procrastination is the art of keeping up with yesterday."

Don Marquis
(American Writer, Columnist, Novelist, Playwright and Poet, 1878-1937)

We all put off doing things from time to time. You and I included. It's human nature to occasionally procrastinate. Procrastination becomes a *problem* when you inhabit this state from one day to the next and find yourself living in a holding pattern.

Procrastination restrains your action and cripples your ability to achieve. Unfortunately *intent does not translate into results.* Neither does indecision or *almost* doing something. The same goes for habitual delays, postponement or deferment.

You simply cannot overcome problems effectively and efficiently when you procrastinate.

I'm not talking about taking the time to appraise your options before making a decision on the best course of action. I'm talking about the inability to make a confident, timely decision and move forward with solving your problem.

You must learn to overcome procrastination before you can problem-solve to the best of your ability. When you can identify the *reason for your procrastination*, you can tackle it logically and rationally.

See whether any of the following causal factors resonate with you.

- ➤ Perfectionism.
- ➤ Fear of making the wrong decision – linked with needing others' approval.
- ➤ Limited self-belief.
- ➤ Negative self-talk.
- ➤ Feeling overwhelmed because you failed to break the problem down into bite sized problems.
- ➤ Lack of commitment to solving the problem due to undervaluing the reward.
- ➤ Fear of success.
- ➤ Activating a subconscious habitual response.
- ➤ Lack of clarity around the problem.
- ➤ Lack of motivation/energy/drive because you feel forced into solving the problem.
- ➤ Fear of failure.
- ➤ Lack of problem solving experience.

Procrastination can be a difficult habit to break. When you change your mindset or take the necessary steps to challenge your causal factor/s, procrastination will lose its power.

This is a process. It will not happen overnight.

Be realistic. Take small steps and aim for improvements, not complete eradication. Be mindful of making changes then slipping back into old procrastinating patterns.

You will need to be on guard and monitor yourself.

Blame

"I like to praise and reward loudly, to blame quietly."
Catherine 11 (Russian Statesman, 1729-1796)

Blame is a negligent problem solving strategy. It holds other people accountable for your problems. Blame shifts responsibility on to others and/or claims the problem is their fault. If you are overcoming your problems by playing the 'blame game', it's time to stop. Playing the blame game is a sign of *your inadequacies.* Let's be honest about this. I know we've all been there at one time or another…some of us more than others. But the reality is there are never any real winners.

➤ Blame breeds resentment, anger, hatred and a host of other very negative emotions.

➤ Blame disempowers. It falsely releases ownership of your problem, but the problem is still a problem and will remain so, until it is acknowledged and resolved.

➤ Blame is an emotion of weakness. It focuses on other people's flaws whilst ignoring your own.

➤ Blame stunts your personal growth with a missed opportunity to develop self-respect, replacing it with shame.

➤ Blame never truly overcomes your problems.

➤ Blame creates further inter-personal problems.

I stopped playing the game a long time ago and as a result, feel so much more authentic. That blame game was eating into my sense of self, my sense of responsibility, my sense of ownership, my sense of power and my sense of truth.

➤ What about *you*?

➤ Are *you* still playing the blame game?

➤ Are *you* still blaming others for your problems?

If so, it's time to step up and take charge of your own problems! Show some courage to yourself and others. When you have a problem, *own* it. That way, you will own the solution as well.

Denial

"And that is how we are. By strength of will we cut off our inner intuitive knowledge from admitted consciousness. This causes a state of dread, or apprehension, which makes the blow ten times worse when it does fall."

David Herbert Lawrence (English Novelist and Poet, 1885-1930)

When the problem you are facing is just too uncomfortable or too difficult to accept, your mind activates the defense mechanism of denial. Denial protects you from hurt, pain or suffering. Denial involves these elements.

- ➤ Rejecting your problem.
- ➤ Insisting that it is not true despite evidence to the contrary.
- ➤ Refusing to acknowledge that you have a problem.
- ➤ Acting as if nothing has happened and all is normal.
- ➤ Wearing a mask.
- ➤ Telling yourself a white lie.

Denial tricks you into believing that if you *don't admit* there is a problem then there isn't one.

If you happen to admit the problem to yourself and nobody else, denial *deludes* you by convincing you that the problem will solve itself. Better still, if you stop thinking about it altogether, the problem will vanish as though it never existed.

The issue with denial is that you *prevent* yourself from overcoming your problem, which stops you from moving forward. In reality, *the problem still exists* at either a conscious or unconscious level. If the problem lives just below the surface, you may be using a lot of energy to keep it at bay. If it lives deep within you, gnawing away silently at your very essence, you may only be aware of the problem when something happens to trigger it into consciousness. Then you are left staring it in the face, with all its ugliness, re-igniting your fears or suffering tenfold.

Learning how to confront denial involves the following.

- ➤ Being *aware* of denial.
- ➤ Asking yourself if you are in denial.
- ➤ Asking yourself why you are in denial.
- ➤ Admitting that your problem feels huge *and* there are ways to manage it.
- ➤ Acknowledging that your problem is painful and dealing with it will also be painful *but you will get through it.*

➤ Asking yourself if denial will benefit you in the long term.

➤ Recognising that denial has never solved a problem and it won't solve yours now.

➤ Recognising that *you can ask* other people for help with your problem.

➤ *Asking for that support.*

➤ Allowing yourself to show emotion about your problem.

➤ Imagining how you will feel when you overcome your problem.

Try not to be fooled by denial. It *appears* to protect you, but in truth it stops you from seeing and solving your problems.

Chapter 8

Looking After Yourself

Your overall health

"Wisdom is to the soul what health is to the body"
Joseph-Rémi Vallières de Saint-Réal (Canadian Judge, 1787-1847)

You are important. Look after *yourself,* or you won't be able to solve anything.

Your health is vital in every area. Pay attention to your physical, emotional, spiritual, and mental health by listening to your mind and body. They will let you know when you need to eat, hydrate, rest, sleep, exercise, play, work and socialise. The signs will be there in the form of weariness, stress, hunger, thirst, exhaustion, illness, boredom, frustration, anger, aches and pains, headaches, depleted energy levels and difficulty thinking clearly, to name a few. Do not ignore these signs. Attend to them!

Your overall health is reflected in your ability to problem-solve *whilst maintaining* a sense of balance and harmony in your life.

Exercise

"It is exercise alone that supports the spirits, and keeps the mind in vigor."
Marcus Tullius Cicero (Roman Statesman, 106-43 B.C.)

Make exercise an important element of your life at any age. The benefits are many. Through exercise, your problem solving abilities are boosted in the following ways.

- ➤ You have more energy because more oxygenated blood is reaching your brain.
- ➤ You can better manage stress because physical exercise serves as an outlet for excess negative energy.
- ➤ Your mood is improved because exercise stimulates various 'feel good' brain chemicals.
- ➤ Exercise is believed to help you get a better night's sleep, heightening your capacity to think with clarity and focus.
- ➤ Your level of strength, fitness, and confidence is increased, helping you to believe in your problem solving abilities.

30 minutes of daily exercise is ideal, but 30-40 minutes 3 times a week will suffice.

Ask yourself the following questions to boost your motivation and exercise choices.

➤ What exercise do *I* already enjoy?
➤ What exercise did *I* used to enjoy?
➤ Which of these types of exercise could *I* enjoy again?
➤ What sort of exercise would *I* like to try?

Here are some ideas to get you started:

rock climbing	water-skiing	snow-skiing
dancing	bowling	boxing
walking	golf	football
table tennis	track and field sports	jogging
skateboarding	fencing	tennis
aerobics classes	swimming	cycling
basketball	yoga	rowing
martial arts	netball	squash
hockey	surfing	cricket
baseball	soccer	going to the gym

Remember, *any* physical exercise is beneficial, even if it's climbing a staircase or taking a short walk around the block.

Keep in mind that when you don't feel motivated enough to exercise *that* is the time to exercise. Exercise will *replenish your energy levels* by getting your blood circulating and oxygenating each cell in your body. You will then be able to tackle your problems with renewed vitality.

Sleep

"There is a time for many words, and there is also a time for sleep."
Homer (Greek Poet, 800-750 B.C.)

Sleep is an essential ingredient in bolstering your problem solving efficiency.

You need to determine the amount of sleep *you need* in order to function at an optimal level. You will likely need between 6-9 hours of sleep per night.

Sufficient sleep brings many advantages.

➤ It helps to lower the level of stress hormones in your body.

➤ It improves your ability to concentrate and think clearly.

➤ It boosts your memory.

➤ It enhances your ability to process, learn and retain new information.

➤ It helps to support your immune system.

Equipped with a good night's sleep, you can get *more done* in your waking hours in *less time*, because your mind is sharp, your thought processes are fast and your concentration levels are raised.

To promote sleep try these strategies.

➤ Exercise your body during the day.

➤ Avoid caffeine before bedtime (and 2 hours prior).

➤ Unwind your mind and body before bedtime.

  ➤ Take a warm bath.

  ➤ Read a good book.

  ➤ Listen to music.

  ➤ Do some deep breathing exercises.

  ➤ Do whatever helps you relax.

➤ Go to bed around the same time each night and wake up around the same time each morning. This will synchronise your body clock and promote a recurring sleep pattern.

Conduct a *sleep audit* on yourself.

Use the following checklist to ensure you are getting sufficient sleep. Be aware that this checklist is not mutually exclusive to a lack of sleep, but it can be used as an *indicator*.

1. Do you often feel tired during the day?

2. Do you yawn a lot?

3. Are you grumpy and irritable for no particular reason?

4. Do you regularly have low energy levels?

5. Do you feel lethargic?

6. Do you frequently fall asleep in a chair or on the couch during the day/evening?

7. Is your thinking 'foggy'?

8. Do you have difficulty remembering things?

9. Do you find it difficult to learn or retain new information?

10. Do you often react emotionally to situations?

11. Do you suffer from poor judgement?

12. Do you get sick regularly – coughs, colds, viruses, infections, feeling 'run-down'?

When running low on sleep or energy levels, remind yourself that the word 'rest' is derived from the word 'restoration'. Adequate amounts of rest and sleep are required to give your mind and body time to cleanse, repair, and revitalise from the inside out. This, in turn, allows you to overcome problems to the best of your mental and physical ability.

When problem solving, be mindful that adequate sleep is not a commodity, it's a necessity!

Eat a balanced diet

"Man is what he eats."

Ludwig Feuerbach (Greek Philosopher, 1804-1872)

Eating a 'balanced diet' means you consume the right types and amounts of food and drink to meet your nutritional needs. A balanced diet will supply the nutrition and energy your body requires to maintain and support cell, tissue and organ functioning. You can consume a balanced diet by eating a wide variety of foods from the basic food groups: vegetables, fruits, grains (breads and cereals), dairy, meat and oils.

An 'unbalanced diet' can cause problems with the functioning and maintenance of your brain and nervous system, which can *compromise* your problem solving ability.

Here are some important tips regarding a balanced diet.

➤ Research and educate yourself about how much of each food group your body needs.

➤ Learn how to read/interpret the nutrition panel and ingredients list of all the foods you eat and look for hidden sources of fats and sugars.

➤ Eat breakfast – it fuels your mind and body at the start of the day.

- ➤ Eat at least three meals each day.
- ➤ Eat at regular time intervals.
- ➤ Eat foods from each of the food groups.
- ➤ Adopt the 5 colour rule – aim for 5 different colours on your plate at every meal.
- ➤ Drink plenty of water throughout the day to hydrate your cells.
- ➤ Eat *fresh* food.

Respect your body and carefully consider the benefits of what you do and don't put in your mouth. Essentially, 'you are what you eat'.

Fresh air

"Water, air and cleanliness are the chief articles in my pharmacopeia."
Napoleon Bonaparte (French Leader, 1769-1821)

How can spending time in the 'great outdoors' assist your problem solving abilities?   The answer lies in the benefits of *breathing* in fresh air.

Fresh air oxygenates all the cells in your body more rapidly and efficiently than stale air, as it contains a higher percentage of oxygen. The more oxygen your brain receives the more clearly you can think (and problem-solve). Fresh air also cleans out your lungs, getting rid of impurities such as dust, and filling them with oxygenated air. Fresh air can help clear your mind, encouraging calmness and composure.

So get outside, surround yourself with nature and breathe!

Relaxation

"Take rest; a field that has rested gives a bountiful crop."
Ovid (Roman Poet, 43 B.C.-17 A.D.)

Being able to relax your mind and body, helps you cope with stress, encourages a restful night's sleep, eases physical and mental tension and induces calm, rational thought.

If you have difficulty relaxing try these suggestions:
- deep breathing
- doing yoga
- meditating
- taking a warm bath
- bathing in essential oils
- having a massage
- having a foot spa
- having a spa bath
- getting a facial
- indulging in a day spa treatment
- lazing around

- laying down and relaxing each muscle group, one at a time (isolate each muscle group, tense the muscles, then let go and relax the muscles)
- closing your eyes and listening to soothing music
- playing with your pet
- visualising
- taking a walk on your own.

Take some time to relax *every day.*

Leisure time/pursuits/hobbies

"All intellectual improvement arises from leisure."
Samuel Johnson (English Author, 1709-1784)

Sometimes work, family, domestic tasks, problem solving and commitments take over your life. You can't consistently perform at your best in these areas without some leisure time.

Leisure time spent pursuing interests or hobbies, brings enjoyment, interest, relaxation, good memories and life balance. You need this outlet. Stop problem solving and lighten up for an hour, a day or a weekend.

You may have many hobbies/leisure pursuits that you enjoy. If so, that's great. Then again you may not. You might need to find some, re-discover some or dabble in some, to discover what brings you pleasure.

Ask yourself the following questions.

➤ What do *I* enjoy doing for fun/pleasure?
➤ What did *I* used to enjoy doing for fun/pleasure?
➤ What have *I* always wanted to do for fun/pleasure?
➤ What would *I* like to try for fun/pleasure?

Refer to the following leisure pursuits and hobbies to get you thinking:

horse riding	painting	car racing
jigsaw puzzles	singing	playing an instrument
cake decorating	motorbike riding	bush walking
playing board games	woodwork	doing up old cars
chess	jewellery making	re-decorating
calligraphy	baking	going to concerts
sailing	sewing/knitting	paint ball
writing poetry	reading crime novels	acting
star gazing	hang gliding	beachcombing
fishing	floral designs	face painting
antique collecting	playing cards	genealogy
dancing	hiking	crosswords
pottery	scrapbooking	join a club

When you spend time on your hobbies and interests, you will resume problem solving with a refreshed, positive mindset!

Re-energise

"Every now and then go away, have a little relaxation, for when you come back to your work your judgment will be surer. Go some distance away because then the work appears smaller and more of it can be taken in at a glance and a lack of harmony and proportion is more readily seen."

Leonardo da Vinci (Italian Artist, 1452-1519)

You need time to recharge your batteries. Overcoming problems can be very draining on your mind and body.

One day and night away can work wonders. Your mind will be more productive after a total break in routine. Step out of your life as you know it.

Enjoy some:

➤ physical space
➤ emotional space
➤ mental space
➤ space from people
➤ space from commitments
➤ space from your daily environment
➤ space from routines.

You could even throw all plans out the window and have nothing planned for a day or two. (It is possible.)

If you can't manage an overnight stay, take a 'daycation' instead. This can be just as beneficial.

You don't have to go away, just take the whole day 'off' and do something you enjoy. (Or do absolutely nothing!)

Do not think about your problems. Plan some time to re-energise right now. Your mind, body and problems will thank you.

Supports

"A friend is a present you give yourself."
Robert Louis Stevenson (Scottish Writer, 1850-1894)

Support people come in all shapes and sizes. They come in all ages. They come from all walks of life. They come from near and far. They come in different capacities; face-to face, in a group setting, via phone or text or email or Skype. They can be who you expect or who you don't expect. They can be someone you know well or someone you've just met. Their involvement can be brief or long term.

Their support can take many forms:
- listening to you
- empathising with you
- talking with you
- bringing you knowledge and experience from a similar situation of their own
- doing the shopping
- doing the housework
- cooking meals
- helping with the children

- being a shoulder to cry on
- taking you out for some fun
- researching, gathering data or information, doing or collating paperwork
- wiping away your tears
- making you smile or laugh
- bringing you coffee (and chocolate).

Anyone can be a support person:
- a partner
- a friend
- a family member
- a neighbour
- a work colleague
- a person from your past
- a volunteer
- someone from an agency
- somebody from a support group.

Whoever they are and however they come to you, embrace them, be grateful for them and let them support you in overcoming your problems.

Seek professional help

"Those that won't be counseled can't be helped."
Benjamin Franklin (American Politician, 1706-1790)

Sometimes you need the support of a professional. Discuss this with your local doctor. They can talk through options such as referral to a counsellor or psychologist. Talking through problems with a professional is a wonderful coping strategy if things are becoming too hard to manage. Applaud yourself for seeking this type of support. It really is a sign of strength to ask for help when you need it!

Keep in mind that accessing the help of a professional does not release you from your problem solving role.

➤ You are still responsible for overcoming the problem.
➤ You must still manage the problem solving process.
➤ You are still the person most familiar with yourself and your problem.

However, with professional help you can feel supported in these areas. At times of difficulty, this type of support can be invaluable.

Chapter 9

Finding the Magnificence in Problems

Opportunities in problems

"Wise men make more opportunities than they find."
Francis Bacon (English Lawyer and Philosopher, 1561-1626)

There are *always* opportunities in problems. They are usually well hidden so you have to look for them carefully. That's what makes them unique. Unlike other opportunities that are much more obvious, opportunities in problems are cleverly disguised between and within your thoughts. They want to be found but they won't reveal themselves. It's your job *to discover them.* The opportunities within your problems will appear when you genuinely ask yourself some quality questions about the *benefits of experiencing your problems.*

1. What have I learnt that I can apply to other areas of my life?
2. What do I need to pay closer attention to in other areas of my life?

3. How can I change for the better?

4. How has my life been enhanced?

5. What can I now do differently?

6. How am I a better person?

7. How can I become an even better person?

8. How can I be a positive influence in the lives of others?

9. What am I grateful for as a result of this problem?

When you realise that every one of your problems holds within it an opportunity of some sort, problems take on a whole new meaning. They become exciting, stimulating, rewarding life experiences. They become part of your blockbuster life.

The opportunities in problems vary in nature. They can offer you the chance to:

- learn something new
- self-reflect
- teach/educate others
- regulate your emotions
- be adaptable
- evolve as a person
- have the courage to live your life fully
- live through pain, becoming stronger as a result
- learn how to ask for help
- see challenges through until the end
- persist against the odds.

Armed with this knowledge and insight, try to be open to your problems. I know it can be difficult, but trust that your problems are an opportunity to *learn* and *grow* in so many ways. The language you use, the questions you ask, your self-talk and your mindset are all paramount in defining your situation and finding opportunities within your problems.

Personal Growth

"Adversity has the effect of eliciting talents which in prosperous circumstances would have lain dormant."

Horace (Roman Poet, 65-8 B.C.)

Overcoming problems serves as a major source of personal growth. Your capacity to achieve and your sense of inner strength become magnified. This spills over into other areas of your life.

As you solve more and more problems, you will discover what wonderful character strengths have been inside you all along. You will also broaden your repertoire of competencies, adding new knowledge, skills and insights, creating an even more capable you. A you, who has amongst other things, become an expert problem solver. A natural by-product of this process is self-development. You will notice growth in the following areas:

- ➤ efficiency
- ➤ awareness
- ➤ being in control of your thoughts
- ➤ asking quality questions
- ➤ self-respect

➤ using new skill sets

➤ having the courage to participate in life

➤ time management skills

➤ wisdom

➤ confidence

➤ knowledge/ learning

➤ resilience

➤ empowerment

➤ responsibility

➤ assertiveness

➤ self-belief.

In my family, as in numerous other families, we have faced many health and medical challenges over the years. As a result, huge amounts of knowledge have been acquired across various areas of health.

The personal growth I have experienced in my efforts to support my family has been staggering. I am not the same person I was fifteen years ago. I am a much better version of myself in every way. This personal growth was not a choice, but a necessity. I was confronted with a 'do or die' situation time and again. Each time I chose 'do'. I continue to choose 'do'.

Your problems can be a vehicle for creating a *better version* of you. Just remove their disguise and uncover *your* opportunities for personal growth.

When you acknowledge and accept that life is a series of ups and downs, problems lose their sting. When you stop expecting life to be fair and get on with living the best way you know how, problems fade from the limelight. When you solve enough problems, particularly complex ones, you realise that what doesn't kill you really *does* make you stronger.

Overcoming Future Problems

"Each problem that I solved became a rule which served afterwards to solve other problems."

René Descartes (French Mathematician, 1596-1650)

As you solve more and more problems in a knowledgeable, structured way, you become better and better at overcoming problems. Future problems are not so daunting. That's because you have the skill set and experience from past problems to draw upon. Many future problems you would have once deemed major, will seem minor. The nature of the problems has not changed. But your ability to solve them has! You have a different *problem solving starting point* to the one you used to have. It's operating at a more sophisticated level and will continue developing as you keep problem solving to the best of your ability, using a series of strategic steps.

In the not too distant future, with many well solved problems behind you, challenges may be welcomed into your life with quiet confidence.

Beyond the problem

"What we have done for ourselves alone dies with us; what we have done for others and the world remains and is immortal."

Albert Pike (American Lawyer, 1809-1891)

Overcoming problems brings with it an opportunity to make a difference. That difference may be for one person, or it may be for many. It may be for the current population or it may be for future generations. It may be for one nationality or it may be for multiple nations.

In my mind, when the outcome of overcoming your problem, be it major or minor, *is making a difference to others*, your problem has been a gift.

Making a difference to others has been the impetus for all my actions beyond my problems. These actions include writing books, writing articles, public speaking, facilitating trainings and seminars, counselling and coaching.

If you want to take action beyond your problem, you *can*! The possibilities for making a difference to others are limited only by your imagination. If you feel strongly enough, extract the message that you want to share from your problem solving experience, then package it in a way so others can benefit.

Your decision to go *beyond a problem* will not only make a positive difference to others, it will also reward *you* with a sense of indescribable purpose!

Chapter 10

All About You

Taking action now

"Never leave that till tomorrow which you can do today."
Benjamin Franklin (American Politician, 1706-1790)

Now that you have access to the tools (knowledge, skills and attitudes) required for overcoming problems, there's only one thing left to do… take action!

Here are some reminders of what you need to do.

➤ Use the *8 steps* – **'ACT TODAY'**.
➤ Apply the *8 steps* to overcome problems of all types – minor, major, painful and complex problems.
➤ Be practical when you problem-solve – allocate time, deal with one problem at a time and keep your problems in perspective.
➤ Be aware of your *thoughts – feelings – actions* so that you can control them.

- ➤ Aim for optimistic thought patterns, positive emotional states and proactive behaviours that will help you overcome problems.
- ➤ Minimise negative thoughts, negative emotional states and unhelpful behaviours.
- ➤ Look after yourself by nurturing your mind and body.
- ➤ Think of your problems as an opportunity to learn and grow.

Right now is a very exciting time for you – it's a time to take action! It's as simple as putting the *8 steps* into place. I know that you can. Feel empowered and go for it!

Living your blockbuster life

"It is never too late to be what you might have been."

George Eliot (English Novelist, 1819-1880)

Knowing the secrets to overcoming problems brings with it the confidence and self-belief that *you really can* live your blockbuster life. (You're already well on the way!)

Remember, you can read and re-read the pages in this book as often as you like. At times you may only need to re-read certain chapters or sub-topics. Use the information as a resource for prompting, guiding, encouraging and directing yourself to take action.

Let the skills and strategies you acquire from overcoming problems lead you to a life of true fulfilment.

Ultimately… *you* are the master of your problems… *you* are the master of your solutions… and *you* are the master of your life. Make it a blockbuster!

"It is the surmounting of difficulties that make heroes."

Louis Kossuth (Hungarian Statesman, 1802-1894)

Be the hero of your blockbuster life!